THE 25-DAY VICE-PRESIDENT

Alabama's Rufus de Vane King

JEFFREY K. SMITH

The 25-Day Vice-President
Alabama's Rufus de Vane King
All Rights Reserved.Copyright © 2025 Jeffrey K. Smith
v2.0

The opinions expressed in this manuscript are solely the opinions of the author and do not represent the opinions or thoughts of the publisher. The author has represented and warranted full ownership and/or legal right to publish all the materials in this book.

This book may not be reproduced, transmitted, or stored in whole or in part by any means, including graphic, electronic, or mechanical without the express written consent of the publisher except in the case of brief quotations embodied in critical articles and reviews.

Outskirts Press, Inc.
http://www.outskirtspress.com

ISBN: 978-1-9772-7901-9

Cover Photo © 2025 Elaine Kerr. All rights reserved - used with permission.

Outskirts Press and the "OP" logo are trademarks belonging to Outskirts Press, Inc.

PRINTED IN THE UNITED STATES OF AMERICA

Table of Contents

FOREWORD i
PROLOGUE v
1   Tarheel born 1
2   Politics and Diplomacy 7
3   Alabama Fever 15
4   Jacksonian Democrat 24
5   Bon Voyage 56
6   Aunt Fancy and Miss Nancy 69
7   Return to Capitol Hill 92
8   Vice-President King 109
POSTLOGUE 120
AFTERWORD 140
WILLIAM R. KING'S LIFELINE 151
TIME LINE OF HISTORICAL EVENTS OCCURING DURING WILLIAM R. KING'S LIFETIME 154
BIBLIOGRAPHY 164
ACKNOWLEDGEMENTS 170
ABOUT THE AUTHOR 172
OTHER BOOKS BY JEFFREY K. SMITH 173

A horse that can count to ten is a remarkable horse, not a remarkable mathematician. Samuel Johnson

If you hold a cat by the tail, you learn things you cannot learn any other way. Mark Twain

The manner in which one endures what must be endured is more important than the thing that must be endured. Dean Acheson

The farther backwards you can look, the farther forward you can see. Winston Churchill

Democracy is the recurrent suspicion that more than half of the people are right more than half the time. E. B. White

Life is like an onion. You peel it off one layer at a time, and sometimes you weep. Carl Sandburg

FOREWORD

The 25-Day Vice-President: Alabama's William Rufus de Vane King represents my 24th overall book and 21st publication in the "Bringing History Alive" series.

The book is written in narrative format, absent endnotes and footnotes. A comprehensive bibliography, however, documents source materials. The author's use of italicized non-proper words is intended to emphasize key points in the story line. Parenthetical sentences are employed to provide additional historical details about individuals or events immediately referenced.

A time line of William Rufus de Vane King's life follows the afterword section. King died 41 days shy of his 67th birthday. During the six plus decades of his life, numerous historical events unfolded and are documented in a separate time line, just prior to the bibliography section.

In the 200 plus years since Alabama's admission to the Union, the state has produced its share of notable, colorful, and controversial politicians. Some are remembered for their forward thinking while others utilized popularity and power to worsen injustices directed toward African Americans as well as the poor, regardless of race.

Bibb Graves was the first person to serve two four-year terms as Governor—1927-31 and 1935-39. Born in Montgomery County's Hope Hull Community, Graves was a Phi Beta Kappa graduate of the University of Alabama. After earning an undergraduate degree in civil engineering, he graduated from Yale School of Law.

Governor Graves was a true progressive who battled against the state's entrenched political machine, commonly referred to as the "Big Mules." The Big Mules were an amalgam of wealthy cotton planters occupying Alabama's prolific cotton-producing Black Belt region and equally affluent financial and industrial magnates residing in the growing city of Birmingham. The two coalitions worked in unison to maintain a firm grip on power, prestige, and enormous wealth. For decades, Big Mules dominated politics on state and local levels, even to the point of routinely handpicking gubernatorial candidates.

Graves' anti-Big Mule, populist agenda included constructing highways and bridges, ending the controversial convict labor leasing program, increasing public education funding for both Black and Caucasian students, raising teacher's salaries, expanding mental health services, promoting women to positions of leadership in state government, establishing the Alabama Department of Public Welfare, providing unemployment insurance, increasing old-age pensions, and supporting organized labor. (Even today, labor unions struggle to establish strongholds in the Deep South). A progressive anomaly in the state of Alabama, Graves vigorously supported President Franklin D. Roosevelt's New Deal programs which were implemented to blunt economic devastation wrought by the Great Depression.

An enemy of wealthy planter and business classes, Graves's core constituency consisted of farmers, blue collar workers, and small business owners. His efforts to assist less-affluent citizens stirred the hearts of enough voters that he became the first individual since ratification of the revised 1901 Alabama State Constitution to twice be elected to four-year terms as Governor. (Even though the 1901 Constitutional

FOREWORD

revision increased Gubernatorial terms from two to four years, electees were not permitted to serve consecutive terms until the 1970s).

James E. "Big Jim" Folsom was a literal and figurative giant in Alabama political lore. The six-foot, eight-inch-tall, 275-pound Folsom was born and raised in Southeast Alabama's Coffee County. Much like Bibb Graves before him, Folsom adopted a populist platform targeted to help "common folks." Governor Folsom increased old-age and welfare pensions, paved farm-to-market roads, constructed new bridges and highways, and increased public education funding. In the era of Jim Crow, Folsom's progressive views on race were far ahead of his time.

Like Graves, Big Jim defied the Big Mules and was elected Governor for two non-consecutive terms (1947-51 and1955-59). If he had not condoned corruption by political cronies, fallen deeper into the abyss of alcoholism, and repeatedly engaged in crude, outrageous public behaviors, Folsom's legacy would be remembered in a more favorable light. (To learn more about the life and times of Big Jim Folsom, please refer to the author's 2022 publication, *A Pea River Progeny*).

George C. Wallace, subject of the author's 2009 biography, *The Fighting Little Judge*, rose to national prominence by employing vicious race baiting as well as defiant opposition to Constitutionally-mandated desegregation of public facilities and suffrage for African Americans. Wallace's dark legacy, fueled by hate, prejudice and intolerance, nonetheless resonated with bigoted whites living in the Deep South and other regions of the country, transforming him into a controversial national figure. Over the course of four decades, Wallace was elected Governor of Alabama four times and launched an equal number of unsuccessful Presidential bids.

As the nominee of the American Independent Party in 1968, Wallace challenged Republican Richard M. Nixon and Democrat Hubert H. Humphrey for the Presidency. Joined by his running mate, retired Air Force General Curtis Lemay, Wallace won 9,906,473 popular votes, 13.5 percent of the total vote, and amassed 45 electoral votes. He also carried five states, Alabama, Georgia, Mississippi, Louisiana, and Arkansas. Though he finished a distant third, Wallace won more popular votes than any third party Presidential candidate to date. Wallace's vote totals were not exceeded until independent candidate H. Ross Perot won 19,741,657 popular votes (18.9 percent) on Election Day 1992. Unlike Wallace, Perot failed to carry a single state and won no electoral votes.

Over the years, Alabama voters have also sent numerous influential statesmen to Washington, D.C., including Congressman Henry B. Steagall and Senator Hugo Black (who was later appointed as Alabama's first and only United States Supreme Court Justice) as well as Senators John Sparkman, Lister Hill, and Richard Shelby. At the 1952 Democratic National Convention, Sparkman was nominated as Democratic Presidential candidate Adlai Stevenson's running mate. Stevenson and Sparkman were defeated in a landslide by World War II hero and Republican Presidential nominee General Dwight D. Eisenhower. California Senator and future President Richard M. Nixon served as Vice President during Eisenhower's two terms, 1953-61.

Alabama, however, has produced only one individual who occupied an office in the Executive Branch of federal government—Vice-President William Rufus de Vane King.

PROLOGUE

As of this writing, 48 people have been elected Vice-President of the United States, beginning with John Adams (1789) and ending with Kamala Harris (2020). Alabama is one of 22 states Vice-Presidents have called home. Vice-President William Rufus de Vane King, however, died only 25 days after he was sworn into office.

A North Carolina native, King was one of two Vice-Presidents born in the Tarheel State. (Vice-President Andrew Johnson was also born in North Carolina but migrated to Tennessee at an early age, before launching his political career). As the son of an affluent, slave-owning planter, King was afforded a quality education, attending elite preparatory academies before matriculating to the University of North Carolina.

After "reading for the law" with a prominent attorney, King passed the bar examination and opened his own practice. However, he was soon drawn toward the world of politics. King was first elected to the North Carolina House of Commons. At the tender age of 25, he won election to the U.S. House of Representatives. From 1801-06, King was a member of the 12th, 13th, and 14th Congresses.

After three terms in Congress, King was hired as Legation Secretary for the American Minister to the Two Sicilies (modern day Italy) and Russia. After serving in the diplomatic corps, King briefly returned to

North Carolina before he and a number of family members migrated to the Alabama Territory's Black Belt region and established themselves as prosperous slaveholding cotton planters. The Black Belt region of Alabama, spanning the width of the uppermost southern region of the state, derived the name from its dark and rich soil conducive to large-scale cotton cultivation.

King soon became a respected local community leader. He worked in conjunction with other prominent residents to develop a new town located on a bluff overlooking the Alabama River. Ab ovo, King named the community "Selma," borrowed from a classic Odessan poem. During the Antebellum-era, Selma, an inland port and hub for cotton distribution, grew to become one of the richest communities in the United States.

Recognized for his leadership abilities as well as past State Legislative and Congressional service in North Carolina, King was elected as a delegate to Alabama Constitutional Convention. During the convention, he was appointed as a member of the select committee responsible from drafting the Constitution, a mandatory step prior to the territory applying for statehood. After admission as the 22nd state to the Union on December 14, 1819, King was elected as one of Alabama's first two United States Senators.

King's first stint in the U.S. Senate spanned 1819-44. During this time, he was appointed to the Committees of Commerce and Public Lands. Respected by colleagues for his for his encyclopedic knowledge of parliamentary procedure, the young Alabamian was elected President Pro Tempore of the Senate in 1836 and remained in that leadership role through 1841.

On April 4, 1841, barely a month after his inauguration, President William Henry Harrison unexpectedly died from pneumonia. By Constitutional mandate, Vice-President John Tyler immediately ascended to the Presidency. At that point in history, President Pro Tempore King automatically became next in line to succeed the new President, if Tyler died or became disabled. For the better part of four years, King was only a heartbeat away from the Presidency itself.

PROLOGUE

In April 1844, King resigned from the Senate after President Tyler appointed him American Minister to France. Fluent in French, King proved to be an excellent negotiator during his two-year assignment in Paris. He successfully convinced France to neither align with Great Britain attempting to prevent the United States from annexing the Republic of Texas nor providing financial and military aid to Mexico during the Mexican-American War

After returning home to Alabama in 1848, King was again elected to the United States Senate. Though he had been out of elective office for four years, King's reputation as a well-respected senior statesman preceded him. Consequently, his transition to the Senate proved seamless.

During the 31st Congress, King served as Chairman of the Committee on Foreign Relations and Committee on Pensions. In 1850, he was once again elected President Pro Tempore of the Senate. By the end of his Congressional career, King had served eight years as President Pro Tempore under five different Vice-Presidents.

On July 19, 1850, President Zachary Taylor died approximately two weeks after contracting a gastrointestinal illness. When Vice President Millard Fillmore succeeded Taylor, President Pro Tempore King again found himself next in line for the Presidency.

Over the course of his political career, King's political affiliations changed, but his agenda remained consistent. At various times, he was elected to office as a Democratic-Republican, Jacksonian Democrat, and mainstream Democrat.

In addition to public service, King was a slave-owning cotton planter who believed involuntary servitude was a Constitutional right. He further supported expansion of slavery into developing western territories. At the same time, King opposed secession, identifying as a Southern Unionist. His opposition to secession made King an anathema to the vast majority of so-called "fire eaters" in the Deep South.

King believed the spread of slavery could be negotiated to the satisfaction of most Southerners and Northerners, save ardent Abolitionists, without dissolution of the country and subsequent armed conflict.

Consequently, he helped draft the Compromise of 1850, one of several legislative initiatives forestalling secession and onset of the American Civil War for nearly a half century.

While most of King's Congressional colleagues respected his soft-spoken manner and leadership skills, some poked fun at his foppish dress and mannerisms. Regularly donning his powdered wig, a distinctly outmoded fashion statement, King appeared unfazed by frivolous fashion critiques.

Many of King's contemporaries, as well as future historians, have repeatedly speculated about his sexual orientation. King's close friendship and lengthy cohabitation with James Buchanan, another prominent statesman and lifelong bachelor, led to rumors about the true nature of their relationship. Rumor and inuendo suggesting the two men were gay lovers has survived for generations. Were those opinions shaped by personal animosity and judgmental biases? Do intimate relationships between consenting adults significantly impact the course of history? The controversial issue of sexual orientation will be subjected to greater scrutiny in the pages to follow.

King's career as U.S. Senator abruptly ended in December 1852, shortly after achieving his long-held dream of being elected Vice-President of the United States. (Alongside King, New Hampshire Democrat Franklin Pierce was elected President). Gravely ill with tuberculosis, King traveled to Cuba after the General Election, hoping the Spanish colony's tropical climate would serve as a palliative treatment for the dreaded illness.

Consequently, King's poor health prevented him from returning to Washington on Inauguration Day. By special disposition from Congress, King took the Vice-Presidential oath in Cuba on March 4, 1853, marking the first and only time in American history a Vice-President or President has been sworn into office on foreign soil.

Less than a month later, King concluded his illness was terminal and further treatment useless. Determined to "die in his own bed," King returned home for the final time. On April 18, 1853, just one day

PROLOGUE

after returning to his southwestern Alabama plantation home, King expired. Consequently, he became the only Vice-President in American history who never returned to Washington, D.C. and occupy his elected seat.

Historians document the "what dids" and contemplate the "what ifs." *The 25-Day Vice-President* not only allows readers to revisit the Antebellum-era but also examines controversial issues of today and yesteryear, including sexual orientation.

While William Rufus de Vane King's impact on history is neither as significant nor well-documented as many of his contemporaries, the North Carolina-born, Alabama adoptee's record as a public servant is admirable and his life journey most interesting.

1

Tarheel born

William Rufus de Vane King, the man destined to become the 13th Vice-President of the United States, was born on his family's cotton plantation in Sampson County, North Carolina on April 7, 1786. His birth occurred only four years after British General Charles Cornwallis surrendered his forces at Yorktown, ending the Revolutionary War, and some two years before the United States Constitution was ratified.

Sampson County was situated in the Coastal Plains of North Carolina, commonly referred to as the Tidewater Region. Located approximately 30 miles west-northwest of the Atlantic Ocean, King's birth county was bounded on the west by the Blue Ridge and Great Smoky Mountains.

The Tidewater's original inhabitants were Coharie Indians. European settlers, most of whom had earlier immigrated from England, Wales, and Scotland, eventually moved to the area. In 1784, the area was officially designated Duplin County, but was later re-named in honor of John Sampson, a prominent member of the North Carolina House of Commons. (When North Carolina's State Constitution was revised in 1868, the House of Commons became known as the State House of Representatives).

Clinton was established as the county seat in 1852, the namesake of Richard Clinton, foster-son of John Sampson. Sampson had originally held title to the land where the town was constructed.

Encompassing 986 square miles, Sampson County's topography was largely flat with occasional small hills dotting the landscape. In addition to swampy forests, yellow grass, wildflowers, and longleaf pines, the sandy soil was suited to sustenance farming as well as large-scale cultivation of cash crops, including cotton, tobacco, peanuts, and rice. Breeding and raising swine and poultry further contributed to Sampson County's agroeconomic output. The manufacture of lumber, furniture, and animal feed also augmented the county's financial livelihood.

Sampson County's residents enjoyed a temperate climate and regularly escaped extreme high and low temperatures during summer and winter months. The area's abundant wildlife pleased naturists and hunters alike. A wide variety of birds commonly flocked to the North Carolina Coastal Plains, adding a pastoral cacophony of sound and color.

The future Vice-President was the third of eight children surviving into adulthood and born to William Rufus King Sr. and Margaret de Vane King over the span of 18 years. Thomas, the eldest, was born in 1779, followed, in order, by Margaret, William Jr., Tabitha, Ann, Helen, Catherine, and John.

William King Sr. was a Revolutionary War patriot and respected community leader. He served as Justice of the Peace and was a delegate to North Carolina's 1778 Constitutional Convention. The elder King was later elected to the North Carolina House of Commons. A member of the slaveholding aristocracy, he earned a lucrative income cultivating cash crops, including cotton and tobacco.

Prior to William Jr.'s birth, the King family had lived in the British colony of North Carolina for more than 60 years. His paternal ancestors hailed from Northern Ireland, and originally settled near the James River in the Virginia Colony before migrating south along the Atlantic Seaboard.

William Jr.'s paternal grandfather and great-grandfather, both named Michael, were family patriarchs. The King family initially resided in Bertie County, North Carolina, near the western end of Albemarle Sound.

When William Jr.'s great-grandfather died, he left behind three sons and daughters, ranging in age from pre-teen to adolescence. For reasons unknown, his widow Isabel asked a family, last name Snell, to take custody of her children. The Snell family and King children eventually relocated to the North Carolina Coastal Plain.

William Jr.'s grandfather later married Mary Catherine, one of the Snell's daughters. Mary Catherine eventually gave birth to 10 children, including William King Sr., who later married Margaret de Vane.

Margaret descended from a prominent French Huguenot family. Huguenots were French Protestants who followed the teachings of famed theologian John Calvin. Under Catholic rule of King Louis XIV, more than 200,000 persecuted Huguenots were forced to leave France and settle in other European countries as well as Africa and North America. Margaret's maternal grandparents were among those who fled to North America.

The expatriated de Vane family first settled in the Maryland Colony before moving to New Hanover, North Carolina, located in the colony's southern coastal region. Shaped like a tornado, New Hanover's narrow land mass jutted southward into the Atlantic Ocean and eventually became home to Carolina Beach and Wrightsville Beach. (The latter was named in honor of the Wright brothers who launched the world's first successful airplane flight on December 17, 1903, along the North Carolina shoreline).

Wrightsville also served as the seat of government for Wilmington County. The de Vane family likely chose North Carolina as their home after receiving a land grant from the King of England in 1735.

According to family lore, 16-year-old Margaret played a bit role during the Revolutionary War. While gathering silk from the family planation, which would later be dyed and sewn into dresses, she was confronted by a British Army officer mounted on horseback. Alarmed that her father and brother were fighting Redcoats at distant locales and fearful for her own well-being, Margaret began screaming.

"Pray, don't be frightened. I am Colonel Caningham of England, one of Lord Cornwallis' staff," the officer consoled the terrified young woman.

Alerted by unexpected commotion, Mary de Vane rushed to defend her daughter and confront the Brit: "What is it you wish, sir?"

After removing his hat and graciously bowing, Caningham replied: "I have been sent by my General to find a suitable place for his headquarters. I think this house will just suit. Who owns it?"

"My husband, Mr. de Vane. But he is not at home this eve," Mary answered, failing to disclose her spouse was an active member of Colonial forces waging war against the British Army.

"Well, madam, if you all act right and behave yourself like ladies, I'll see that you are treated like ladies. But if you try to cause us any trouble, you will learn what trouble really is," the Colonel calmly but firmly explained.

"I will try quietly to submit with the best grace I can," Mary replied.

For two weeks, General Cornwallis established his headquarters in the de Vane's home. While their family home was occupied by the enemy, Mary recalled "she and her daughter were treated with the greatest respect."

Later in life, Margaret would marry William King Sr. The young couple had no way of knowing their third-born child would grow up to become a prominent 19th Century statesman.

William King Jr. was a rambunctious child, but at the same time, thoughtful, intelligent, and perceptive. He answered to the name William Jr., so as not to be confused with his father. Early in their lives, the King children were taught proper social graces by their parents and expected to display exemplary manners.

William Jr. and his boyhood friends enjoyed playing soldiers, often reenacting major Revolutionary War battles. Using sticks for swords, they particularly enjoyed staging imaginary cavalry charges against General Cornwallis' redcoats.

While his young son was playing soldier, William Sr. became an affluent member of the Tarheel State's planter class. Tax and census records from 1790 documented personal ownership of 31 slaves, fifth among all slaveholders residing in Sampson County. When William Jr. reached age 21, his father gifted him with more than 1,000 acres of rich farm land and numerous slaves to work the fields. Ever enterprising, the elder King purchased additional slaves, raised cattle, and operated a sawmill.

A child of privilege, William Jr. was afforded a quality education. He attended preparatory school at Grove Academy, an institution chartered by the North Carolina State Legislature in 1786. Located in nearby Kenansville, the Grove Park Presbyterian Church operated the boarding school. Boys and girls from throughout the state matriculated to the academy and studied a classic curriculum, including science, mathematics, Greek, and Latin. Even though he attended a Presbyterian school, William, Jr. and his family were confirmed Episcopalians.

Later, William Jr. enrolled at Donaldson Military Academy in Fayetteville, approximately 30 miles from his hometown. The school took pride in providing "the best in military training for the young men of the Fayetteville area."

When he was 13 years old, William King Jr. transferred to the Preparatory School in Chapel Hill where his brother, Thomas, was already enrolled. Just two years later, the precocious lad was admitted to the University of North Carolina.

The youthful collegian joined the Philanthropic Society, one of the university's two esteemed literary and debate clubs. As an active member of the prestigious society, King held numerous positions, including councilor, supervisor, and president. He soon established enduring friendships with fellow society members, John A. Thornton and John H. Eaton, the latter destined to become Secretary of War during

President Andrew Jackson's Administration.

Ever studious, King also possessed defiant and mischievous streaks. Along with Thornton, he was reprimanded for not only missing Philanthropic Society meetings but also for laughing aloud during staid gatherings. Fellow classmates clearly recalled the time King, ever the prankster, swiped a bee hive from a local apiarist during the dead of night.

At age 18, a year prior to graduating, William Jr. left the University of North Carolina to "read for the law" under William Duffy, a respected lawyer and jurist who lived in Chapel Hill. In that era, it was not uncommon for prospective attorneys to serve educational apprenticeships rather than seek admission to America's limited number of accredited law schools. King not only pored over text books selected by Duffy but also learned to write legal briefs, draft contracts, and prepare wills. He further benefited from observing and mimicking his mentor's court room acumen and polished social skills.

While serving his apprenticeship, King's innate defiance led to a run-in with local authorities. After failing to show up for jury duty in Sampson County, he was fined 20 shillings (approximately 40 modern day dollars) and received an official reprimand. The embarrassing lesson was timely; King never again disregarded an obligatory court summons.

In late 1808 or early 1809, King was admitted to the North Carolina bar. As an attorney and member of the wealthy planter class, King, like his father before him, became a respected community leader.

From that point forward, public service would largely define William Rufus de Vane King's legacy.

2

Politics and Diplomacy

After admission to the bar, King opened his law practice in Clinton, North Carolina. Eager to participate in community activities, he completed rites necessary to become a Free Mason and joined Phoenix Lodge Number Eight in nearby Fayetteville. Within three years, King had advanced to the rank of Master Mason.

With land and slaves given to him by his father, King began adulthood as a man of means. He soon occupied a position in the state's planter class aristocracy.

In 1808, King broadened his circle of friends and acquaintances when summoned for a tour of duty in the local militia. State militias were progeny of the historic "minutemen," first organized by American colonists in 1776. Coalitions of minutemen were formidable fighting forces opposing the British Army during the Revolutionary War. Colonial-era militiamen earned their names after boasting they could muster arms with only a minute's notice.

The militia unit King joined had proudly defended Wilmington, North Carolina, during the American Revolution. During King's militia service, however, no foreign or domestic enemies threatened the country. He did, however, emerge from the experience with a life-long moniker, "Colonel King." (In the era of King's service, militiamen were permitted to elect their own commanding officers).

In 1806, King's popularity, patriotism, and leadership skills helped propel his election to the North Carolina House of Commons. At that point in history, each county in North Carolina was represented in the legislative branch of state government by two Representatives and one Senator. Candidates seeking election to the House of Commons were required to own at least 100 acres of land, and if elected, consent to serve their first one-year term without pay.

In 1807, 21-year-old King traveled by horse-drawn carriage to the state capital in Raleigh, approximately 64 miles north-northeast of Clinton. Maintaining sufficient popularity with his constituents, the young lawmaker was re-elected in 1808.

While serving in the House of Commons, King not only helped craft statewide legislative proposals but also supported the national policies of President Thomas Jefferson. Like Jefferson, King was a member of the Democratic-Republican Party and joined the President in opposing unwanted and aggressive intrusions by Great Britain and France in America's foreign and domestic affairs.

In 1809, before completion of his second term in office, fellow lawmakers elected King to serve as a solicitor (district attorney) in North Carolina's Superior Court. As chief prosecutor, King represented the state's Piedmont Region, located between the eastern Coastal Plains and western mountains. Traveling between courthouses in Raleigh, Greensboro, High Point, and other cities, King established influential connections essential to future political advancement.

In 1810, an opportunity emerged for King to ascend the political ladder. Thomas S. Kenan, having served five consecutive terms in the U.S. House of Representatives, decided not to seek re-election in North Carolina's 5th Congressional District. King, who resided in that district, immediately decided to run for the open House seat.

While campaigning, King took the high road by focusing on

his agenda rather than attacking opponents' policies and potential character flaws. Close friend and fellow North Carolinian, Robert Strange, proudly recalled King "was not a man to stoop to the arts of demagogue."

King's strategy proved effective when he triumphed at the polls. Only 24 years old and less than a year shy of the Constitution's minimum age requirement for U.S. Congressmen, King was forced to wait until November 1811 before occupying his seat.

King's freshman House class included two men destined for future notoriety, South Carolina's John C. Calhoun and Henry Clay of Kentucky. While King's name was not widely recognized outside the halls of Congress, the young North Carolina lawmaker diligently labored on behalf of his constituents. Twice re-elected, King remained in office from 1811-16, serving in the 12th, 13th, and 14th Congresses.

Soon after King joined Congress, the nation confronted a major international crisis. Less than 30 years after winning the Revolutionary War, the United States was on the brink of another armed conflict with England.

President James Madison was particularly aggrieved by the British Navy's impressment of English-born crewmembers working aboard American military and merchant vessels at sea. The British government justified impressment by refusing to recognize individuals born on native soil as true American citizens. To enforce this policy, British warships regularly menaced trans-Atlantic trade routes between the United States and Europe.

In addition, the Brits were actively aiding Native Americans repeatedly attacking white settlers in North America's western frontier. (Some historians, however, blame expansionist-minded Americans of deliberately provoking England. If the U.S. emerged victorious in war, England could well be forced to relinquish rule over Canada).

After economic sanctions against England proved unsuccessful, King and many Democratic-Republican colleagues, aptly named "war hawks," pushed for aggressive action. In contrast, Federalist Party lawmakers, many of whom were Anglophiles, opposed war with England.

The conflict eventually intensified to a point of no return. On June 1, 1812, Madison asked Congress to approve his declaration of war against England, the first time in history an American President proposed such action. Seventeen days later, the Senate passed the President's declaration by a vote of 19-13. The House of Representatives also approved the measure, 79-49. The War of 1812, also known as the "Second War of Independence" and "Mister Madison's War" would last for two years, seven months, four weeks, and two days.

While fighting battles on the home front and in Canada, the United States was aided by a handful of Native American allies, including Choctaw, Cherokee, Lower Creek, and Seneca tribes. A larger coalition of Native Americans, fearing continued westward expansion of American settlers would further displace them from tribal lands, sided with England. Tecumseh's Confederacy as well as Sauk, Potawatomi, Wyandot, Dakota, Red Stick, Winnebago, Ojibwe, and Caughnawaga Mohawk tribes joined forces with invading redcoats.

The war generated predictable hero worship. Two prominent Generals, Andrew Jackson and William Henry Harrison, would later be elected U.S. President. (The pattern of nominating successful military leaders to run for President would continue well into the 20th century).

Despite considerable bellicosity, America was ill-prepared for war. On the night of August 24, 1814, the British Army captured Washington, D.C. after defeating American forces at Bladensburg, Maryland. Enemy soldiers set fire to nearly every public building in the District of Columbia, including the White House and Capitol. Private residences were also burned to the ground during the siege.

The War of 1812 officially ended when American lawmakers ratified the Treaty of Ghent on February 17, 1815. The United States, however, had paid a steep toll: 2,200 killed in action, 5,200 deaths from infectious diseases, 4,500 wounded, and nearly 20,000 surrendered to redcoat invaders. The Brits also shared in the misery: 10,000 deaths from war wounds and battlefield infections, with an additional 15,500 combatants surrendering as prisoners of war.

The war essentially ended in a draw. All conquered territories were returned to their rightful owners. To the displeasure of American expansionists, England maintained rule over Canada. War hawks nonetheless bragged America had proven capable of withstanding invasion from a hostile foe.

When lawmakers returned to Washington, D.C. for the September 1814 Congressional session, they were shocked to discover much of the city lay in charred ruins. Congressman King's own rented residence was among those destroyed by invading British soldiers. Consequently, he was forced to relocate to a different boarding home, which he shared with a small contingent of Southern Congressman as well as Vice-President Elbridge Gerry.

Gerry, a 70-year-old native of Massachusetts, was among the country's founding fathers. After serving in the pre-Revolutionary War Continental Congress, he was elected to Congress during a brief period of unsustainable governance established by the Articles of Confederation. After ratification of the U.S. Constitution, Gerry won election to the U.S. House of Representatives and later served as Governor of his home state.

From March 4, 1813, until his death on November 23, 1814, Gerry served as the fifth Vice-President of the United States during President James Madison's second Administration. The term "gerrymandering" became his lasting namesake. Gerrymandering occurs when Congressional districts are disproportionately reconfigured to favor a given political party or benefit a certain class of voters. Gerry was elected to Congress after a Massachusetts voting district was deliberately redrawn to include larger numbers of voters supporting his policies.

Even though he was a North Carolina slaveholder, King established close bond with non-Southern politicians. While briefly cohabitating with Gerry, King "enjoyed a long intimacy" with the Vice-President and "derived much knowledge from his long experience in public affairs." The two men also shared outmoded tastes in fashion. When Gerry donned his own powdered wig, King was subjected to fewer teasing barbs from his contemporaries.

Congressman King faithfully supported President Madison's Democratic-Republican Party initiatives. As a member of the Southern planter-class aristocracy, King supported States' Rights, including expansion of slavery into developing western territories. Like most Southern lawmakers, he opposed the National Bank and high protective tariffs. King and fellow opponents of the National Bank were fearful of placing excessive power in the hands of the federal government. In addition, elevated tariffs deliberately inflated costs of imported products coveted by Southerners whose economies were agrarian-based.

Throughout his tenure in Congress, King rented rooms at boarding houses alongside fellow lawmakers. After dinner, King and his roommates often gathered in the parlor to socialize and discuss politics. On occasion, members of a boarding home clique would visit or host lawmakers cohabitating elsewhere.

Those living under the same roof tended to be politically cohesive. In 1812, King had joined most of his fellow boarders in voting to declare war against England.

Young, handsome, and single, King actively participated in Washington, D.C.'s lively social scene. An aimable and entertaining conversationalist, he was regularly invited to formal dinners and other soirees.

First Lady Dolley Madison later recalled the North Carolina Congressman's attendance at a White House function: "Mr. King came sans ceremonie, and gayly chatted with us until dinner was served."

Questions soon arose concerning King's sexual orientation. Some observers noticed he appeared more comfortable around men than women. Others were puzzled by the young lawmaker's bachelorhood. Rumors about King's sexual proclivities would follow him for the remainder of his life.

On November 4, 1816, King unexpectedly resigned from Congress to become Secretary of the U.S. Legation to the Kingdom of the Two Sicilies, encompassing Sicily and a sizeable portion of southern Italy. (The entire region would eventually become known as Italy).

King served under Foreign Minister William Pinkney, a ready and able mentor. The resourceful 52-year-old Maryland native had initially studied medicine before entering the political arena.

A skilled orator, Pinkney was one of America's earliest diplomats. President George Washington sent him to London to negotiate payment for damages inflicted by British military forces on American properties during the Revolutionary War. In 1804, President Thomas Jefferson once again dispatched Pinkney to England, where he served as Foreign Minister for seven years.

By the time King was hired as Legation Secretary, Pinkney's resume was expansive. In addition to diplomatic posts, he had served as a U.S. Congressman from Maryland on two separate occasions, Mayor of Annapolis, Attorney General of Maryland, and U.S. Attorney General during President Madison's Administration. Later in life, Pinkney would be elected to the U.S. Senate.

Pinkney was also a decorated veteran of the War of 1812. On August 24, 1814, during the Battle of Bladensburg (Maryland), Major Pinkney was wounded in combat.

Thirty-year-old King, having never travelled abroad, welcomed an adventure under Pinkney's tutelage. Before departing the U.S., King began a private journal. Like many Americans traveling outside the country, he regularly documented his observations and experiences in writing.

"Actuated by a desire to visit the continent of Europe which I had fostered from a very early period in my life … I determined to resign my situation in Congress," King wrote in one of his first journal entries, neglecting to mention he may have also feared losing his re-election bid after voting in favor of an unpopular pay raise for Congressmen and Senators.

An eager King agreed to pay his own travel fare when the trans-Atlantic voyagers set sail from Annapolis, Maryland. During his year abroad, King not only learned diplomatic skills but also became fluent in French; both would serve him well in the future.

Eager, hard-working, and sociable, King was a valuable aide to the American Foreign Minister. In addition to coordinating Pinkney's correspondence and scheduling, King was also keeper of the official diplomatic record. According to historian Albert Pickett, King used his time well, "making himself acquainted with the institutions of various governments and the condition of their people."

After the Foreign Minister settled indemnity cases involving the Kingdom of the Two Silicies, Secretary of State James Monroe sent Pinkney to Russia in hopes of negotiating a commercial treaty. Impressed by his Legation Secretary's efficiency and work ethic, Pinkney dispatched King to St. Petersburg in advance of his own arrival.

"Colonel King, who knows perfectly my views, will supply verbally what be deficient in this letter," Pinkney wrote Russian diplomats.

King's advance preparations were successful. In January 1817, Pinkney wrote President-Elect Monroe that he was "graciously received" by Russian royalty.

In late summer 1817, King abruptly resigned his position. In a letter to John Quincy Adams, Monroe's successor as Secretary of State, Pinkney explained his Legation Secretary "quitted me on his return to the U.S."

Why did King suddenly depart Russia? Was it the result of a rumored unrequited love affair? Did he consider his mission was complete after Pinkney failed to negotiate a trade agreement with Russia? Or was King merely homesick? (Those questions will be addressed in greater detail in a subsequent chapter).

After returning home, King would join thousands of others migrating to North America's growing western frontier.

3

Alabama Fever

William King Sr.'s health rapidly deteriorated to the point of no return while his namesake was serving abroad in the diplomatic corps. Separated from his family by the Atlantic Ocean and reliant upon notoriously slow communication channels, William Jr. did not learn of his father's death for several weeks. As the second oldest son, 30-year-old King would be expected to assume a patriarchal role within the family.

At some point prior to King's return to America, his older brother, Thomas, relocated from North Carolina to the Alabama Territory, where he purchased land and established a cotton plantation along the Black Warrior River near the west-central town of Tuscaloosa. Thomas wrote his younger brother about the land rush to the Alabama Territory, also known as the "westward migration of the cotton culture," and "Alabama Fever." He also encouraged his male sibling and other family members to join him in a cotton planter's paradise.

The Alabama Territory was originally occupied by an estimated 15,000 Native Americans, including Creek, Chickasaw, Cherokee, and Choctaw tribes. As a result of European colonization in the Western Hemisphere, the area was claimed by the Spanish Empire, which ruled from 1565-1763. After the Treaty of Paris was signed in 1763, ending the French and Indian War as well as the Seven Years War between

Great Britain and France, the area that would later become known as Alabama became a protectorate of the British Empire.

On April 17, 1798, after the United States emerged victorious in the Revolutionary War and took control of lands south of Canada and east of the Mississippi River, Congress created the Mississippi Territory. Commonly referred to as the "Old Southwest," the Mississippi Territory consisted of millions of acres north of the 31st parallel, previously claimed by the state of Georgia.

By 1804, settlers had established two prominent communities in Mississippi Territory, St. Stephens on the southern portion of the Tombigbee River (the southwest corner of present-day Alabama) and Natchez on the eastern bank of the Mississippi River. Not surprisingly, Native Americans were enraged when white settlers began displacing them from generational homelands. The Red Stick Creeks, namesake of the tribe's favorite clubbed weapons, the "red sticks of war," instigated violent reprisals against the encroachment.

On July 27, 1813, Red Sticks, led by half-Native American Chief Peter McQueen, attacked white soldiers and settlers in the southern portion of the eastern half of the Mississippi Territory. During the so-called Battle of Burnt Corn, Red Stick warriors killed two Americans and wounded 15 others. On August 30 of that same year, approximately 1,000 Red Sticks under the command of McQueen and William Weatherford, also known as Lamochatte and Red Eagle, attacked Fort Mims, a stockade located 40 miles north of the port city of Mobile. The infamous Fort Mims Massacre left 265 militiamen and 252 settlers dead. The Red Sticks also took nearly 100 African American slaves captive.

In response to what were deemed unprovoked attacks, General Ferdinand Claiborne mustered additional militiamen from the Western Mississippi Territory. General Andrew Jackson also marched his Tennessee militiamen southward to attack belligerent Native Americans.

The ensuing Creek War lasted less than a year, as firearm-wielding militiamen decimated Red Stick combatants. In August 1814, under auspices of the Treaty of Fort Jackson, General Andrew Jackson forced the Creek Confederacy to cede more than 21,000,000 acres in southern portions of Georgia and the future Alabama Territory. Native Americans who had not died in battle or succumbed to previously unencountered infectious diseases transmitted by white soldiers and settlers were forcibly relocated to the west, leaving behind a ruling society of white men in the Mississippi Territory.

Affluent plantation owners, aware the territory could sufficiently accommodate two future pro-slavery states, petitioned Congress to set the wheels in motion. Consequently, on December 10, 1817, the Mississippi Territory was formally split—the western portion was admitted to the Union as the state of Mississippi while the eastern half was designated the Alabama Territory.

St. Stephens served as the Alabama Territory's first capital city. Further north, near the Tennessee state border, settlers were busy founding the city of Huntsville. William Wyatt Bibb, a migrant from Georgia, was appointed by President James Monroe to serve as Alabama's Territorial Governor.

Settlers from Tennessee, Georgia, South Carolina, and North Carolina continued to migrate to the Alabama Territory at lightning pace. In 1810, less than 10,000 non-Native Americans occupied the area. By 1818, the population had increased to nearly 68,000.

Southern plantation owners were eager to feed ever-growing demands for cotton in domestic and international markets. Those who settled in the Alabama Territory's Black Belt region were particularly fortunate. The dark, sticky soil, filled with rich deposits of clay capable of holding moisture in place for extended periods, was perfectly suited for large-scale cotton cultivation.

William R. King Jr. realized Alabama Fever presented not only an opportunity to increase his wealth but also established a new launch pad for his political ambitions. Consequently, he lobbied on behalf of his friend, Israel Pickens, who was appointed Receiver of Public Lands in the newly created Alabama Territory. In October 1818, King purchased 780 acres in the Alabama Territory from the federal land office in Milledgeville, Georgia.

Other family members joined King's westward migration, including his sister Margaret, who was married to John Beck, and sister Tabitha, wife of Basil Kornegay. While King and his relatives sold all landholdings in North Carolina, they took their slave laborers with them. Family members purchased land tracts in the Alabama Territory's Dallas and Marengo Counties. Within four decades, the Kings would own upwards of 500 servants, ranking them among the largest slaveholders in Alabama.

King's Black Belt bottom land was in southwestern Dallas County, adjacent to the Alabama River which snaked from the north and east before merging with Tombigbee River, 45 miles north of the port in Mobile. The Tombigbee eventually relinquished its waters to the navigable Mobile and Tensaw Rivers which emptied directly into the Gulf of Mexico. King christened his planation, located less than 10 miles upriver from the town of Cahaba, King's Bend.

Cahaba, the closest community to King's plantation, had a most interesting existence. While Alabama was still a territory, St. Stephens and Huntsville served as the first and second seats of government. After Alabama achieved statehood. Cahaba, sometimes spelled Cahawba, was designated as the *temporary capital city*. The rather obscure site was selected as a concession to South Alabama Constitutional Convention delegates in exchange for their willingness to compromise on apportionment of state legislative districts.

Located at the confluence of the Cahaba and Alabama Rivers, the small but vibrant community was expected to grow into a metropolis. If those plans had come to fruition, Cahaba might have remained the state's permanent seat of government.

Built atop a 16th Century Mississippi Indian village, some locals believed Cahaba was "haunted" from the beginning. Haunted or not,

Cahaba was most definitely located in a flood plain. After torrential downpours, the Alabama River was prone to overflowing and submerging adjacent lowlands. In 1825, after repeated episodes of flooding, the state capital was relocated further north. Tuscaloosa, sometimes spelled Tuskaloosa in honor its native American roots, became Alabama's *first permanent capital.* (In 1846, Montgomery became the present-day seat of state of government).

After losing its designation as state capital, Cahaba rapidly declined. During the Civil War, the dying town served aa a prisoner of war camp, housing approximately 3,000 captured Union Army soldiers. In 1865, after yet another flood, the Alabama State Legislature moved Dallas County's seat of government from Cahaba to nearby Selma.

By 1870, Cahaba's population had shrunk to 300, and many businesses and residences had rotted, burned, or were completely dismantled. At the turn of century, Cahaba was completely deserted, even though it would not be officially unincorporated until 1989.

Today, Cahaba is a popular destination for those exploring ghost towns. The Old Cahawba Archaeological Park houses a visitor's center and museum as well as walking paths leading to structural ruins, cemeteries, and other supposedly haunted spots.

Utilizing slave labor, King built a plantation home at King's Bend. According to different sources, he named his house Chestnut Hill or Chestnut Grove. (Chestnut Hill is the name most often cited.). Constructed atop the highest ground available on his plantation, King hoped the residence would escape flooding from the Alabama River's overflowing banks.

Abundant flora surrounded King's Bend's cotton fields and home site. Chestnut trees, whose straight trunks and hardwoods were ideal sources of construction lumber, were commonplace. (Before the end of the 19th Century, chestnut blight would kill millions of chestnut trees in the United States).

King's chestnut tree-lined driveway strayed from the main dirt road and led to a cul-de-sac directly in front of his home. While not the grandest of Antebellum-era manors, King's one-story, rectangular-shaped dwelling was sizeable and tastefully designed. Several columns supported the veranda leading to the house's formal front entrance. When King wanted privacy from visiting family and friends, he would enter the house through a separate, less ornate side door. The surrounding homestead contained a shed-covered deep well, a free-standing office building, smokehouse, the plantation overseer's headquarters, and numerous slave cabins.

In addition to King's Bend, he purchased additional smaller cotton plantations, including acreage in neighboring Lowndes County. According to 1860 land records, various King family members owned a total of 2,436 acres in Dallas County alone.

More land holdings meant increased cotton cultivation and additional manpower. Consequently, King grew more dependent on slave labor. In 1820, he owned 20 slaves. By 1853, the number had increased to 180.

King no doubt played a role in perpetuating the barbaric institution of slavery and monetarily benefited from the labors of human chattel. While there is no silver lining inside the dark cloud of slavery, King was nonetheless regarded as *more humane* than many plantation owners and was not known to administer cruel punishments to his slaves.

King freely shared his home with family members who regularly visited King's Bend. He also readily acclimated to the patriarch role for his younger kin. King developed a warm relationship with his niece, Margaret Eliza Beck, daughter of sister Margaret King Beck, who had died of unknown causes in 1822. Just two years later, Margaret Eliza's father, John Beck, also passed away.

"I have the greatest confidence, and my affection for you is unbounded," King wrote his orphaned niece.

King's closest and most enduring bond was with Catherine

Margaret Parrish, young daughter of his sister, Catherine King Parrish, who died during childbirth. Catherine Margaret's father, Harvey Ellis, a State Legislator and one-time Mayor of Tuscaloosa, also expired at an early age. After she was orphaned, King treated Catherine Margaret like she was his own child. Uncle and niece remained companions and confidants the remainder of his life.

Little time passed before King was recognized as a man of distinction is his adopted home. His polite demeanor, previous service in Congress, diplomatic experience abroad, and leadership skills caught the attention of influential local residents. Consequently, King played a major role in establishing a new town in the Black Belt region.

Before eventual abandonment, Cahaba, located six miles downstream from Chestnut Hill and on the Alabama River, was the nearest community to King's plantation. Given Cahaba's propensity for flooding, King and other area residents concluded Dallas County's future prosperity necessitated construction of a new town positioned on higher ground.

King and six other local leaders seized the initiative by establishing a town land company. The group ultimately selected a bluff on the Alabama River near King's plantation as a location for building the proposed town.

In years past, the site had been home to a Mississippian Native American tribal city. An Indian burial mound remained a tangible tribute to the past. Some historians believe the Native American community was called Piachi and marked the actual location where 16th Century Spanish explorer and conquistador Hernando de Soto crossed the Alabama River during his westward trek.

Located above the flood line, the bluff overlooked a potential deep water river port. The newly constructed town would eventually become a hub for shipping Black Belt cotton via barge to Mobile and the

Gulf of Mexico for widespread sale.

The community was christened Moore's Bluff before King proposed a change: "I would like to name this town Selma. In my studies, I came across a Scottish poet name Ossian who wrote an epic poem entitled *The Songs of Selma* which has become one of my favorites. In the poem, Selma means 'high seat' or 'throne,' and as the location sits high above the river, I think high seat would be quite appropriate." (Ossian was a legendary bard who penned poems about a group of warriors, the Fianna Eireann, and their leader Finn MacCumhail. In 1762, Ossian's name became well known throughout Europe when Scottish poet James Macpherson published the bard's works. The term Ossian is also used to describe the rhythmic style of Macpherson's own prose).

The remaining members of the town land company agreed with King's proposed name change. In the Antebellum-era, when cotton was king, Selma grew to become one of the most affluent municipalities in the U.S.

On July 5, 1819, King was among 44 delegates from 22 counties who convened in Huntsville at the Alabama Constitutional Convention. Drafting a State Constitution was mandatory before any territory could apply for statehood. Fellow delegates elected King Chairman of the Committee of Fifteen, the group responsible for drafting the actual document.

Contemporary historian Albert Pickett was not surprised King was elected chairman: "In all relations of his life, Colonel King has maintained a spotless reputation. His frank and confiding disposition, his uniform courtesy and kindness, has endeared him to numerous friends, and commanded for him the respect and confidence of all who have had the pleasure of his acquaintance."

On December 14, 1819, Alabama was formally admitted as the 22nd state in the Union. Territorial Governor William Wyatt Bibb was elected to the same position in the newly established state. The State Legislature rewarded King's leadership by electing him one of Alabama's first two U.S. Senators.

John Campbell, a fellow convention delegate, was among those who admired King's leadership skills and ability to negotiate compromises. Campbell informed his brother King possessed "some very fine qualities, and I cannot but feel gratified in seeing him occupy any situation he wishes."

Campbell, however, was less enamored with Alabama's other U.S. Senator, John W. Walker. Compared to King, Campbell found Walker "amazingly spoilt."

Just two years after migrating from North Carolina to Alabama, William R. King was headed to Washington, D.C. to represent his adopted state on the national level.

4

Jacksonian Democrat

When William R. King returned to Capitol Hill, now representing the state of Alabama, he again sought lodging in boarding houses. His roommates were mostly Southern lawmakers, including Samuel Smith (Maryland), Philip Pendleton Barbour (Virginia), and John Bell (Tennessee). Many lawmakers occupying boarding houses were bachelors or widowers. Others did not possess the financial means to maintain separate households and were forced to leave wives and children at home during Congressional sessions. Consequently, co- or multi-habitation by male lawmakers in Washington, D.C. was a routine occurrence. King's personal and political enemies, however, would eventually make much ado about his living arrangements.

In the nation's capital, King found political differences were much like those on the state level. In Alabama, King's so-called "North Carolina Faction" opposed the "Georgia Faction," also known as the "Broad River Group" or "Royal Party."

The conflict between Alabama politicians centered around financial policies. While the North Carolina Faction supported establishment of a designated State Bank, their Georgia counterparts preferred depositing state revenues in private financial institutions. King, however, would later modify his position and oppose rechartering the National Bank.

King was particularly annoyed by outside meddling which conflicted with his political ambitions. In 1818, Georgia Senator William H. Crawford offered his considerable political influence to help King secure a much-coveted position as a land receivership officer based in Huntsville, but only if the Alabamian would refuse to seek election to the U.S. Senate once the territory became a state. A perturbed King, however, refused to snap the Georgian's dangling bait.

Four years later, when King sought election to a full six-year Senate term, Crawford once again attempted to reshape political dynamics in his sister state. He offered to lobby the President to appoint King as an American Minister to a South American country if he agreed to leave the Senate. King once again declined to alter his career trajectory and was re-elected to Congress. An angry King eventually confronted Crawford about his meddlesome manipulations.

"The proceedings in relation to them, have produced, or give full document to, feelings of great acerbity towards me, in the bosom of Wm. R. King," Crawford wrote to a friend after the scolding. King and Crawford would later reconcile to maintain cohesiveness within the Southern faction of the Democratic-Republican Party.

When America was in her infancy, President George Washington warned against the divisiveness of ideological partisanship. While Washington established many time-honored traditions adopted by future Presidents, he was unable to prevent establishment of competing political parties. For the entirety of his career in public service, King would not only encounter hostility from opposing political parties but also mediate intraparty squabbles.

On Capitol Hill, King was a skilled lawmaker. Unlike many colleagues, King was open to compromise, even concerning the thorniest of issues. He chose to model conciliatory leadership rather than partisan rancor.

"He was distinguished by the scrupulous correctness of his conduct. He was remarkable for his quiet and unobtrusive, but active, practical usefulness as a legislator. He was emphatically a business member of the Senate, and without ostentation, originated and perfected more useful measures that many who filled the public eye by greater display and commanded the applause of the listening Senate," a fellow lawmaker wrote.

King not only refrained from calling attention to himself but also refused to deliver lengthy, tedious speeches on the floor of the Senate. Both practices endeared him to a great many colleagues.

A master at parliamentary procedures and rules of order, King had little patience for those who spoke often but said little. Kentucky Senator Henry Clay noted King was "as serious as an undertaker at a funeral."

During his first term, King was elected Chairman of the Senate Committees on Public Lands and Commerce. In 1836, recognized for diligence and keen knowledge of legislative rules, King was elected by his peers to serve as President Pro Tempore of Senate. He would remain in that leadership position for five consecutive years. By Constitutional mandate, the Vice-President also served as President of the Senate. If the Vice-President was absent or incapacitated, the President Pro Tempore fulfilled all his legislative duties, including signing bills, administering Constitutional oaths, and presiding over the Senate.

At that point in history, the President Pro Tempore of the Senate occupied a different position in Executive office hierarchy. If the President died, resigned, or was impeached and convicted, the Vice-President automatically ascended to the Presidency. In such a situation, the President Pro Tempore became first in line to succeed the new President. (Today, the President Pro Tempore of the Senate stands third in line of succession to the Presidency, preceded by the Vice-President and Speaker of the House).

As President Pro Tempore, King received praise for his leadership skills. A fellow Senator described him as "warm-hearted," "even-tempered," and an "excellent presiding officer." The same peer further noted King displayed "sound judgment and rich experience" but "could be stern when public interests or his personal honor required it." At the conclusion of his first term as President Pro Tempore, King's colleagues passed a unanimous resolution of appreciation, specifically citing his "ability" and "impartiality."

Approaching middle age, King's appearance and demeanor were more austere. Several fellow lawmakers nicknamed him the "Chesterfield of the Senate" and "Alabama's Chesterfield." Philip Dormer Stanhope, the Fourth Earl of Chesterfield, was an 18th Century diplomat, statesman, and scholar. A century later, American politicians continued to regard Lord Chesterfield as the most genteel of role models.

Throughout his legislative career, King firmly believed Senators should behave with dignity and remain attentive to details. He further regarded compromise as a gift rather than a weakness In 1837, King proclaimed the Senate was "the great conservative body of this republic," but warned "the demon of faction should find no abiding place." For the good of the country, King believed lawmakers should be willing to give and take to pass meaningful legislation benefiting a majority of their constituents.

While King began his political career as a Democratic-Republican, by the mid-1820s, he had evolved into a full-fledged Jacksonian Democrat. (With the passage of time, Jacksonian Democrats evolved into modern-day Democrats). Fragmentation of the Democratic-Republican Party and birth of the "Age of Jackson" were in large part precipitated by the controversial 1824 Presidential election.

Born near the border of North and South Carolina (at various times, both states have staked claim to his birth site), Andrew Jackson was a fighter from the start. After Jackson's father, mother, and two brothers met untimely deaths at early ages, the future President's fiercely independent streak was set in stone.

At age 13, Jackson joined a militia company to fight for American independence during the Revolutionary War. After Jackson was captured by enemy forces, a British Army officer ordered the young prisoner of war to polish his boots. When Jackson flatly refused to demean himself, the Brit struck him with his saber. For the remainder of his life, Jackson bore the swordman's scars on his head and arm as prideful symbols.

Jackson was a man of honor, even to the point of recklessness. It is believed he participated in more than 100 duels during his adult life. Jackson only shot and killed one man, but he also spent much of his life with dueling opponents' bullets lodged in his chest and arm.

Like King, Jackson read for the law in North Carolina before migrating westward. He ultimately settled in the territory later to become the state of Tennessee. After being elected delegate to the 1796 Territorial Constitutional Convention, Jackson helped draft the governmental framework necessary for Tennessee's admission as the 16th state to the Union. Some contemporaries even credited Jackson with choosing the name Tennessee.

Jackson was unanimously elected Tennessee's first Congressman. While serving in the U.S. House of Representatives, he supported the Democratic-Republican policies of party leader and America's first Secretary of State, Thomas Jefferson. After Vice-President and Federalist Party Candidate John Adams defeated Jefferson in the 1796 Presidential election, a disappointed Jackson refused to seek re-election to Congress.

After U.S. Senator William Blount was impeached by the House of Representatives and convicted by the Senate for conspiring with Great Britain to seize the Louisiana Territory from Spain, the Tennessee State Legislature elected Jackson to fill his vacant seat. Once again restless in the role of lawmaker, Jackson resigned from the Senate in 1798, having served only a few months.

After returning to Tennessee, Jackson was elected a State Superior Court Judge. For the next six years, Judge Jackson earned the well-deserved reputation as a no-nonsense jurist who delivered swift and harsh penalties to convicted criminals.

Ever combative, Jackson enlisted in the Tennessee State Militia. In 1802, fellow militiamen elected him Major General. In that era, militia ranks were often based on popularity rather than promotion criteria. (Jackson was no doubt an adept commander. During the Civil War, however, both Union and Confederate Armies discovered *elected* officers often proved to be disastrous military leaders and this practice came to an end).

As a military man, Jackson achieved national fame for engineering victories against the Creek Indians as well as British forces in the War of 1812. His most notable triumph came at the Battle of New Orleans, occurring on January 18, 1815.

The Battle of New Orleans was fought approximately five miles southeast of the downtown French Quarter and home to the modern-day suburb of Chalmette, Louisiana. The engagement was the culmination of England's so-called Gulf Campaign, an ambitious goal to capture Western Florida, New Orleans, and the Louisiana Territory.

British Major General Edward Pakenham and his second in command, Major General Samuel Gibbs, led the attack against forces commanded by Brevet Major General Andrew Jackson. In addition to militiamen, the Americans were aided by 52 Choctaw warriors and French privateer and pirate Jean Lafitte and his raiders.

While the British Army had superior numbers, their attack plan was poorly executed, leaving them vulnerable to ambush. In less than 45 minutes, Jackson's forces decimated the enemy. The Brits suffered 2,037 casualties—291 killed, 1,262 wounded, and 484 missing or captured. Generals Pakenham and Gibbs were among those killed in action. In sharp contrast, the defenders sustained only 71 casualties—13 dead, 39 wounded, and 19 missing or captured.

Interestingly, the Battle of New Orleans occurred 15 days after the Treaty of Ghent was signed, formally ending the War of 1812. News of the pact, signed in Europe, had not yet reached Louisiana prior to the armed engagement.

In 1821, President Monroe appointed 53-year-old Jackson to serve as Territorial Governor of Florida. In October 1823, having earlier declined an offer to serve as American Minister to Mexico, Jackson was once again elected to the U.S. Senate by the Tennessee State Legislature.

A year later, the restless war hero was nominated for the Presidency by non-partisan delegates at the Pennsylvania State Convention. Over the course of 16 years, Jackson's political ascension had been nothing less than remarkable.

During the 1824 Presidential election, none of the candidates ran under established party labels. Jackson's opponents included Senator William H. Crawford of Georgia, Secretary of State John Quincy Adams (a native of Massachusetts and son of the second President of United States), and Kentucky Congressman Henry Clay.

King was an unqualified Jackson supporter. He shared the Tennessean's distrust of big business, disdain for high protective tariffs, opposition to the National Bank, support of America's westward expansion into unsettled territories, and increased purchase of public lands by settlers. Accompanied by fellow boarder and North Carolina U.S. Senator Nathaniel Macon, King traveled to the Tarheel State and campaigned on behalf of Jackson.

When Presidential ballots were tabulated on Election Day 1824, Jackson appeared to be the victor:

CANDIDATE	POPULAR VOTES	ELECTORAL VOTES
Andrew Jackson	153,544	99
John Quincy Adams	108,740	84
William H. Crawford	46,618	41
Henry Clay	47,136	37

Even though he won the most popular and electoral votes, Jackson failed to secure a necessary majority in the Electoral College. Consequently, Article II of the United States Constitution tasked the House of Representatives with selecting the next President. Each state was allocated one vote decided by consensus of its Congressional delegation.

By Constitutional mandate, Clay, who won the fewest electoral votes, was forced to drop out of the race. The Kentucky Congressman, however, would exert considerable influence over the outcome of the election. Clay was in position to catapult Jackson or Adams into the Presidency by "throwing his votes" to either candidate.

On January 9, 1825, Clay met for a "confidential interview" with Adams. The nature of their discussion was so private that Adams, a renowned diarist, made no mention of the exchange in his private journal. Soon afterwards, Clay encouraged his pledged electors to pressure their individual Congressmen to vote for Adams.

On February 9, 1825, the House of Representatives convened to elect the next U.S. President. Adams ultimately triumphed, winning 13 states, compared to seven for Jackson and four for Crawford.

Adams ecstatically wrote in his diary: "May the blessings of God rest upon the event of this day!"

Supporters of Jackson and Crawford immediately cried foul, alleging Adams and Clay negotiated a "corrupt bargain." Those charges were amplified after the President-Elect appointed Clay Secretary of State.

An infuriated Jackson shared his thoughts about Clay's apparent self-serving machinations: "The Judas of the West has closed the contract and will receive the 30 pieces of silver."

For the next four years, Jackson was a man on a mission, plotting revenge against Adams and Clay. In 1825, the Tennessee State Legislature nominated him for the Presidency, *three years* before the next election. Soon after, Jackson resigned his seat in the U.S. Senate and focused almost exclusively on the 1828 Presidential election, officially adopting the party label of *Democrat*.

In one of the first "campaign tours" by a candidate seeking national office, Jackson traveled to Louisiana to commemorate the 30th anniversary of his well-publicized victory against British forces at the Battle of New Orleans

THE 25-DAY VICE-PRESIDENT

In November 1828, Andrew Jackson was elected the 7th President of the United States. He defeated incumbent John Quincy Adams, now affiliated with National-Republican Party, by 139,222 popular votes and dominated the Electoral College, 178-83.

(Two years later, Adams was elected to the U.S. House of Representatives by voters in his home state of Massachusetts. Adams, who "abhorred slavery," achieved Northern acclaim after leading a successful fight to repeal the "gag rule" in 1844. The gag rule, officially introduced by Southern lawmakers, heretofore banned introduction of anti-slavery proposals in Congress).

Adams was still serving in the lower chamber of Congress when he suffered a stroke at his desk on the House floor in February 1848. Unconscious, the 80-year-old Congressman was carried to the office of the Speaker of the House and remained in a coma until his death three days later. Having served in public office during the administrations of the first *11* Presidents, *Adams was the first ex-President elected to Congress, and to date, the only one to serve in the House of Representatives*).

Andrew Jackson's election to the Presidency proved bittersweet. His wife Rachel, a corn-cob-pipe-smoking, homespun product of the frontier, dreaded exposing herself to widespread scrutiny as First Lady. Shortly before Jackson departed for Washington, D.C., Rachel died from natural causes.

"I'd rather be a door-keeper in the house of God than live in that palace," she confided to a friend shortly before her death.

The grieving President-Elect not only blamed himself for his wife's death but also castigated political enemies who had publicly accused Rachel of bigamy after she married Jackson before the divorce from her first husband was finalized. In reality, Rachel mistakenly believed her previous marriage had legally ended before wedding Jackson. More than three years after their initial betrothal, Rachel remarried Jackson trying to rectify the manufactured scandal.

By Inauguration Day, 61-year-old Andrew Jackson, infected with tuberculosis and carrying bullets inside his body from past gun fights, appeared gaunt, frail, and older than his stated age. Despite his unhealthy appearance, Jackson was sworn into office as President in March 1829, and served two full terms with characteristic stubbornness and uncompromising will.

※

King was among many dedicated Jacksonian Democrats. Along with the President, he steadfastly opposed high protective tariffs which made it more costly for mostly agrarian-based Southerners to purchase imported goods. Consequently, King voted against the Tariff Acts of 1824 and 1828.

Out of respect for fellow Southerners, when South Carolina threatened to nullify all federal tariffs in 1832, King voted against Jackson's Force Bill, fearful of giving the President such "tremendous power."

The tariff conflict arose after John C. Calhoun, Jackson's first-term Vice-President and native of South Carolina, proclaimed any state had the right to *selectively enforce* federal laws. Calhoun and his supporters further proclaimed nullification opened the door for states to secede from the Union.

Our Federal Union, it must be preserved," Jackson countered, publicly rebuking his Vice-President.

The tariff argument reached its climax shortly after President Jackson was elected to a second term in November 1832. The incumbent had easily defeated Henry Clay, outpolling his challenger by 157,313 popular votes and winning the Electoral College, 219-49. Less than a month after Jackson's re-election, the South Carolina State Legislature voted to nullify tariffs and threatened to secede from the Union if the federal government attempted to collect any such revenues after February 1, 1833.

Jackson did not respond well to ultimatums, especially in the wake of Vice-President Calhoun resigning from office and winning election as a home state U.S. Senator. Consequently, the President issued a Proclamation on Nullification in December 1832.

"Disunion by armed force is treason," Jackson boldly asserted.

The President began mobilizing U.S. Army troops in preparation for waging war against rebellious South Carolinians. After he threatened to hang former Vice-President Calhoun, Palmetto State lawmakers wisely avoided calling Jackson's bluff by prolonging their secession deadline.

Despite King's opposing vote, Congress passed the Force Bill. The legislation authorized the President to employ troops as a means of enforcing collection of federal revenues. In a rare Jacksonian spirit of compromise, the law provided Southerners some relief by implementing a phased reduction in tariffs. The potential for civil war ended when the South Carolina State Legislature voted to rescind nullification legislation on March 15, 1833, the same day as President Jackson's 66th birthday.

As a native Southerner, King played a key role in negotiating passage of the Tariff Act of 1833, lessening tensions between the federal government and South Carolinians. The Alabama Senator firmly established his reputation as a *Moderate* Democrat and proved to be an effective conciliator between Northern and Southern factions of the party.

While Jackson was miffed by King's opposition to the Force Bill, he nonetheless respected his skills as a negotiator and continued to rely upon his leadership in Congress. Jackson uncharacteristically failed to hold a personal grudge against King and continued to welcome the Alabamian to White House political and social functions.

On the issue of Native American rights, King walked in lock step with Jackson. Both men supported forced removal of Indians from their native lands to pave the way for occupation by white settlers.

King supported expansion of settlements into Ohio, the Northwest Territory, and Missouri Territory, collectively referred to as the expanding Western Frontier. Unlike many Southerners, the Alabama Senator encouraged land purchases by *both pro- and anti-slavery settlers.*

King had earlier voted in favor of the Land Act of 1820 which was enacted into law on July 1 of that year. The legislation was beneficial to settlers who defaulted on their loans after the Financial Panic of 1819.

The Land Act ended the practice of settlers purchasing public domain lands on credit or via four-year installment plans. Instead, up-front land sales became more affordable after the minimum price-per-acre dropped from $2 to $1.25 and the minimum size of land tracts was reduced from 160 to 80 acres. Consequently, settlers' minimum total payments for smaller homesteads dropped from $320 to just under $100.

Desirous of acquiring existing Creek tribal lands in northwestern Alabama, King steadfastly supported ratification of the Treaty of Indian Springs, whereby Native Americans sold 3,000,000 acres to the state. The original treaty, signed on February 12, 1825, was ratified by the Senate a month later. However, when lawmakers discovered Native Americans had been defrauded, the original pact was nullified. After the Senate passed the Treaty of Washington in 1827, Native Americans retained lands previously sold to Alabama. An infuriated King characterized the revised pact as a "villainous fraud." Determined to promote white colonization, King would never be a Native American ally.

King maintained close relationships with his supporters in Alabama, including Governor Israel Pickens. In 1825, Pickens selected King to head up a welcoming committee honoring Revolutionary War hero, French General Marquis de Lafayette, during his forthcoming visit to Alabama. After Lafayette made it known his stay in Alabama was pleasurable, King was lauded for his organizational skills.

A year later, following the death of U.S. Senator Henry Chambers, the Alabama State Legislature elected Governor Pickens to fill the vacant seat. Already suffering from tuberculosis, Pickens served in the Senate only a few months before resigning. Pickens subsequently traveled to the Cuban coastal town of Matanzas, where the island's tropical climate and salt air were thought to be beneficial in slowing progression of active tuberculosis. After palliative treatment failed to work, Pickens died in Cuba in April 1827.

King was saddened by the loss of his friend and benefactor. He did, however, retain sufficient popularity with State Legislators to merit re-election to the U.S. Senate on three consecutive occasions—1828, 1834, and 1840.

***

As a committed Jacksonian Democrat, King opposed a bill to re-charter the Bank of the United States in 1832. Like the President, King believed the centralized National Bank was not only a byproduct of political partisanship but also susceptible to corruption. The controversy surrounding the National Bank would eventually erupt into an historic free-for-all.

As a first-time delegate to the 1832 Democratic Party National Convention, King was appointed to the Committee on Rules. King and other committee members shepherded passage of a new rule whereby Presidential candidates must secure a *two-thirds majority* rather than a *simple majority* of delegate votes to win the party's nomination. (The simple majority rule was reinstated during the 1936 Democratic National Convention when Franklin D. Roosevelt successfully sought re-nomination for the second of his four consecutive Presidential terms).

Throughout his first stint in the U.S. Senate, 1820-44, King's political ambitions steadily grew. At the 1824 Democratic-Republican Convention, he was gratified and astonished after receiving a single vote for the Presidential nomination. King, however, had earlier concluded his ultimate prize was the Vice-Presidency.

***

Frustrated and angered by John C. Calhoun's controversial and premature resignation from the Vice-Presidency, Andrew Jackson engineered the nomination of Martin Van Buren as his 1832 running mate. The incumbent President was certain Van Buren, unlike Calhoun, would remain loyal throughout his second Administration.

Much like Jackson, Van Buren came from humble beginnings. Born in 1792, he was the son of a tavern owner and farmer who resided in the predominately Dutch community of Kinderhook, New York. Standing five-feet, six-inches-tall with a balding dome offset by unruly tufts of hair along the sides and back, Van Buren was a fastidious dresser. He was considered a self-made man who achieved success through determination and hard work. Politically astute, Van Buren earned the nickname "Little Magician." In addition to his personal drive and political acumen, he was also regarded as humble and likeable.

Educated as a lawyer, Van Buren also developed an abiding interest in state and local politics. He eventually became the acknowledged leader of New York's "Albany Regency" political machine. In 1812, Van Buren was elected to the State Senate. His work ethic was most impressive; during his final three years as a state lawmaker, Van Buren simultaneously served as New York's Attorney General.

In 1821, the New York State Legislature elected Van Buren to the U.S. Senate. (Election of U.S. Senators by popular vote was not mandated until ratification of the 17th Amendment on April 8, 1913). Like King, Van Buren was an ardent supporter of Andrew Jackson. When Old Hickory was elected President in 1828, he rewarded Van Buren by appointing him Secretary of State.

During Jackson's first Administration, rifts developed within his Cabinet. Vice-President Calhoun, former U.S. Congressman and Senator, one-time Secretary of War, prior Secretary of State, and John Quincy Adams' Vice-President, harbored aspirations of adding the Presidency to his already impressive political resume. In manipulative fashion, Calhoun tried to convince other Cabinet members to shift their loyalties from Jackson to him. As a result, the Secretary of State became the President's closest advisor. Compared to Calhoun, Jackson lauded Van Buren as "a true man with no guile."

While Calhoun was fomenting discontent within the Cabinet, Van Buren devised a clever solution to outwit the Vice-President. When Van Buren and Secretary of War John Henry Eaton agreed to resign from office suddenly and unexpectedly, remaining Cabinet members felt obliged to follow suit. Van Buren's political calculation enabled Jackson to appoint loyalists to fill the Cabinet vacancies.

Jackson graciously sought to reward Van Buren by appointing him American Foreign Minister to Great Britain. Vice-President Calhoun, angered by the former Secretary of State's disruption of his political cabal, cast the tie-breaking vote denying Van Buren's confirmation as Foreign Minister.

Calhoun's vengeance ultimately backfired, transforming the Little Magician not only into a martyr but also Jackson's second term Vice-President. In 1836, the last year of his two-term Presidency, an ever-popular and powerful Jackson handpicked Van Buren to succeed him.

For reasons unclear, King never honestly liked or respected Van Buren. After amassing considerable support for the Vice-Presidency prior to the 1836 Democratic National Convention, an ambitious King was willing to overlook existing personal and political differences if he could serve as Van Buren's running mate.

Van Buren, however, preferred Kentucky Congressman Richard Mentor Johnson for second spot on the Democratic ticket. Nicknamed "Old Dick," Johnson was a war hero credited with killing Shawnee warrior Tecumseh at the Battle of Thames during the War of 1812. By 1836, Johnson not only enjoyed name recognition but also had the powerful backing of President Jackson.

King could only hope Johnson's major liability, a scandalous sexual relationship with his African American mistress, Julia Chinna, would prevent him from winning the nomination. In an era when race-mixing was decidedly taboo, Johnson's political enemies coarsely nicknamed him the "Great Amalgamator." Despite this controversy, the full backing of Jackson and Van Buren was enough to secure the Vice-Presidential nomination for Johnson. In the fall General Election, Johnson's presence on the ticket resulted in Van Buren losing his running mate's home state of Tennessee where voters were decidedly less progressive-minded when it came to race-mixing.

In November 1836, Van Buren defeated three candidates running under the banner of the up-and-coming Whig Party, U.S. Senators Hugh Lawson White of Tennessee, Daniel Webster of Massachusetts, and William Henry Harrison of Ohio. Van Buren won 50.9 percent of the popular vote and 170 electoral votes. The remaining 111 electoral votes were split among the Whig candidates.

When the U.S. Senate convened to formally certify the Electoral College votes, President-Elect Van Buren's majority was solid. Johnson, however, had only won 143 votes, one shy of a majority. By provision of the 12th Amendment, the Senate was tasked with selecting the next Vice-President. President Pro Tempore King, despite his disappointment at being bypassed for the Vice-Presidential nomination, graciously lobbied colleagues to vote for Johnson. In doing so, King put his national political ambitions on hold until the 1840 election.

During his March 1837 inaugural address, Van Buren cited the "American Experiment" in democracy as a role model for other countries. Within three months, the so-called Financial Panic of 1837 dampened the new President's optimism.

While the 19th Century was marked by cyclical "boom and bust" economic periods, former President Andrew Jackson's financial policies likely contributed to the 1837 crash. After Jackson refused to charter a Second Bank of the United States, restrictions on inflationary lending policies and overall regulation of state banks lessened. As a result, credit was easily obtainable, resulting in uncontrolled land speculation, particularly in the rapidly developing western frontier.

During the last year of his Presidency, Jackson issued a Specie Circular executive order to lessen issuance of credit. The mandate required all purchases be transacted with "hard money," either gold or silver.

To Van Buren's great misfortune, the Financial Panic of 1837 occurred after his predecessor vacated office. Before the economic downturn ended, thousands of Americans lost their homes and properties while hundreds of banks and businesses failed. America's worst financial crisis to date lasted nearly five years.

President Van Buren's anti-inflation policies proved to be of little benefit. Believing easy credit led to reckless business practices and wild land speculation, the President was determined to set a responsible example by keeping the federal government financially solvent. Like his predecessor, Van Buren opposed chartering a Second National Bank of the United States, and for a time, continued depositing federal funds in state banks. The President eventually convinced Congress to pass the Independent Treasury Act of 1840 which established the nation's first government-controlled treasury system.

From that point forward, federal funds were stored in government-controlled vaults rather than state financial institutions or a single National Bank. While King and other Democratic lawmakers blocked establishment of a Second National Bank, they were unable to prevent partial repeal of the Independent Treasury Act of 1840.

The subsequent Independent Treasury Act of 1846 set in motion long-standing governmental financial policies. The law mandated all public revenues be deposited in vaults in the Treasury Building in Washington, D.C. or sub-treasuries located in designated cities. In addition, the Treasury Department paid out its own funds independent from private banks. All monies received or paid out by the country were to be in the form of specie or treasury notes. Even today, the U.S. Treasury continues to oversee all governmental financial transactions. In 1913, a separate entity, the Federal Reserve System, was created to regulate the amount of money circulating in the economy, promote national financial stability, ensure the "safety and soundness of private financial institutions", and promote "consumer protection and development."

During the 1837 financial crisis, Van Buren's fiscally conservative policies included defunding national internal improvements. Consequently, the federal government sold tools slated for use in public works projects. (Van Buren's program of reduced government spending was diametrically opposed to the New Deal public works projects instituted by President Franklin Delano Roosevelt in the 1930s to combat massive unemployment and poverty wrought by the Great Depression).

JACKSONIAN DEMOCRAT

In addition to the troubled economy, Van Buren alienated himself from many Southern Democrats by opposing annexation of the Republic of Texas, a fertile ground for expansion of large-scale cotton cultivation and slave labor. The President, however, feared annexation would lead to war with Mexico.

Leading up to the 1840 Democratic National Convention, King once again set his sights on the Vice-Presidential nomination. Consequently, he sought endorsements from fellow lawmakers, including his closest friend and boarding house roommate, James Buchanan.

Buchanan, who had previously been appointed America's Foreign Minister to Russia in addition to his impressive Congressional service resume, believed he was more than qualified to serve as President of the United States. The two friends began fantasizing about a Buchanan/King national Democratic ticket.

In the end, Buchanan was unwilling to challenge incumbent Van Buren and appeared content to promote King's Vice-Presidential candidacy, as reflected in a letter to John Randolph Clay, his former Legation Secretary: "For my own part, I prefer Colonel King of Alabama. I believe he would add much more strength to Mr. Van Buren in the South & South Western (sic) States, especially in North Carolina of which he is native."

"As a lady, however, possessing, as I know, the Colonel's esteem in an eminent degree, I thought you might reciprocate it by speaking a kind word for him among your friends & particularly among the sex who rightfully govern mankind," Buchanan penned to their mutual friend Eliza Violet Gist Blair.

During Congressional recess, King wrote Buchanan thanking him for his support: "I cannot but feel grateful at the lively interest you manifest."

In early 1840, Alabama State Democratic Party delegates nominated

King as their choice for Vice-President. With Buchanan's assistance, Pennsylvania's State Democratic Party also nominated King.

King had reason to be hopeful about his Vice-Presidential prospects. Since the Presidency of Thomas Jefferson, it was customary for incumbents to select new running mates when seeking a second term. This tradition took root as the result of first-term Vice-Presidents dying in office, irreconcilable political differences between the President and Vice-President, or the incumbent President's desire to add a fresh face to the ticket.

In addition to King, other prominent Democrats were interested in the Vice-Presidency. All prospective nominees assumed Van Buren would follow the established trend by jettisoning Richard Johnson. Secretary of State John Forsythe of Georgia, Senator Robert Walker of Mississippi, and current Governor and Former Speaker of the House James K. Polk of Tennessee were among those interested in replacing Johnson.

Among the five candidates, Polk appeared to have a leg up on his competition. He headed into the convention with an endorsement from iconic Andrew Jackson, a fellow Tennessean, who had earlier decided it was time to replace Richard Johnson on the Democratic ticket.

Tennessee Congressman Aaron Venable Brown also played a significant role in facilitating Polk's political ascendancy. Forty years old, Brown coupled his stern countenance with a matter-of-fact communication style. Born in Virginia, he shared more commonalties with King than Polk. Brown had not only attended the University of North Carolina but also joined the Philosophic Society. And like King, Brown read for the law under the supervision of a well-respected attorney. He was also a slaveholder who migrated westward seeking greater fame and fortune. While King relocated to Alabama, Brown settled in Tennessee.

Unfortunately for King, Brown's close personal and professional relationship with Polk outweighed shared life experiences. After establishing a law partnership with Polk, Brown was elected to the State Senate followed by the U.S. House of Representatives. (Later in life, he would serve as the 11th Governor of Tennessee and U.S.

Postmaster General).

While serving in Congress, Brown developed enmity against both King and James Buchanan. He believed the two lawmakers' close relationship and lengthy cohabitation were suspicious and perhaps "unnatural."

After learning Polk had received Andrew Jackson's endorsement and Brown's unbridled support, King saw the handwriting on the wall and withdrew his name from consideration as a Vice-Presidential nominee. Democratic delegates in Alabama and Pennsylvania subsequently shifted their support to incumbent Vice-President Johnson.

King was no doubt disappointed by yet another missed opportunity to seek the Vice-Presidency. In public, however, he rather disingenuously professed the Senate was "fully equal to my highest ambition."

In private, King bitterly complained to his niece, Catherine Margaret Ellis, that Polk "had thrust himself forward." From that point forward, he viewed Polk and his chief promoter Aaron Venable Brown with considerable disdain.

Even before Brown's salacious rumor-mongering, King had been accused of political collusion. In March 1840, *The Lancaster Examiner*, Buchanan's home town newspaper, reported "intrigue was going on between Mr. Buchanan and William R. King of Alabama, in which Buchanan was to secure the nomination of King to the Vice-Presidency; and King, in return, was at a proper time, to secure the vote of Alabama to Buchanan for the Presidency."

All speculation about the Democratic Vice-Presidential nominee came to a halt when Van Buren refused to cast aside Vice-President Johnson. The incumbent President mistakenly believed Johnson's heroic military record would match accolades afforded the Whig Party's presumed Presidential front-runner, General William Henry Harrison.

When the Democratic National Convention convened in Baltimore on May 5, 1840. Van Buren easily won renomination. However, neither Johnson nor Polk could muster the $2/3^{rd}$ majority necessary to secure the Vice-Presidential nomination. By parliamentarian rules, Johnson had won a plurality of delegate ballots and was retained as

Van Buren's running mate.

As expected, Whig Party National Convention delegates nominated Harrison for President, overlooking renowned statesmen like Henry Clay and Daniel Webster. Harrison, a resident of Ohio, was the hero of the 1811 Battle of Tippecanoe, where he commanded U.S. Army forces to victory over Native American warriors. (Shawnee leaders at the Battle of Tippecanoe included Tecumseh and his brother, Tenskwatawa, also known as "The Prophet"). Harrison earned additional accolades as an Army General during the War of 1812. Convinced Harrison was the best choice to head the party ticket, Whig delegates achieved regional balance by nominating former Virginia Senator John Tyler for the Vice-Presidency.

Whig Party candidates posed formidable challenges to Democrats in the 1840 Presidential and Congressional elections. Founded in 1834 by opponents of Andrew Jackson and his Democratic acolytes, the Whigs remained a viable national party for 20 years.

Henry Clay is most often credited as the founder of the Whig Party. One of the most influential statesmen of the 19th Century, Clay was born in Virginia in 1777. After earning a law degree from the College of William & Mary, he settled in Lexington, Kentucky.

A Democratic-Republican before turning Whig, Clay was elected to the Kentucky State Legislature in 1803. Seven years later, he won a seat in the U.S. House of Representatives and served for 22 consecutive years. In 1811, Clay's colleagues elected him Speaker of the House.

While never a war hawk, Clay patriotically supported President James Madison's declaration of war against Great Britain in 1812. Two years later, he also assisted in negotiating the Treaty of Ghent which formally ended the War of 1812.

While serving as Speaker of the House, Clay initiated the "American System," a federally funded means of improving the nation's infrastructure. In direct opposition to the polices of Andrew Jackson, Clay supported the National Bank and higher protective tariffs, the latter designed to help American manufacturers.

Christened the "Great Compromiser," Clay was the driving

force behind Congressional passage of the Compromise of 1820 and Compromise of 1850, both of which tempered pro- and anti-slavery passions, forestalling the Civil War for four decades. In addition to State Legislator and U.S. Congressman, Clay's prolific career of public service included appointment as John Quincy Adams' Secretary of State and a 16-year stint as U.S. Senator. While he never met the "Great Compromiser" in person, Abraham Lincoln cast his first Presidential ballot for Clay. Lincoln, who became known as "Great Emancipator" while serving as President during the Civil War, described Clay as the "beau ideal of a statesman." (If Clay had not died in 1852 at age 75, many historians speculate he may have engineered further Congressional compromises and delayed onset of the Civil War).

While Jacksonian Democrats portrayed Whigs as aristocrats, the party's membership was quite diverse, including members from different socioeconomic classes and residents of the North and South alike. Senator Daniel Webster of Massachusetts, Virginia Senator and future President of the U.S. John Tyler, New York Senator William Seward, and Pennsylvania Congressman Thaddeus Stevens were among prominent lawmakers who joined the Whig Party.

By opposing Jacksonian Democrats, Whigs reestablished a true "second party system" in America. Democrats dissatisfied with Andrew Jackson's autocratic leadership and former members of the little known Anti-Masonic Party were among those who came to identify as Whigs.

Some Whig party members were evangelical Protestants motivated by enacting moral reforms. Others were ardent anti-slavery Abolitionists. Many Whigs were particularly offended by Jackson's indifference toward Native Americans as white settlers actively migrated to the western frontier. In 1830, after signing the Indian Removal Act, Jackson clearly ignored key facets of the legislation by removing the Cherokee Nation from Georgia to Indian Territory west of the Mississippi River—the infamous "Trail of Tears."

While resenting Jackson's iron-fisted rule, Whigs nonetheless believed in a strong federal government. To better understand the Whig Party's rise to power, it is necessary to revisit controversies surrounding the National Bank.

The National Bank of the United States was a steady fixture in early American history. Alexander Hamilton, the nation's first Secretary of the Treasury, proposed formation of a centralized financial institution for management of federal funds. In 1791, both houses of Congress concurred with Hamilton's recommendation and passed legislation establishing the First Bank of the United States. Following advice from his Secretary of the Treasury, President George Washington signed the bill into law.

The National Bank was charged with depositing tax revenues, loaning necessary funds to the federal government, moving money around the country through its branch networks, and paying bills owed by the government. Private citizens and foreign interests were also allowed to make deposits and take out loans from the Bank of the United States. From the beginning, several prominent statesmen who opposed an all-powerful central government, including Thomas Jefferson, the nation's first Secretary of State and third President, maintained the National Bank was unconstitutional.

As a Jefferson disciple, President Andrew Jackson believed the National Bank was a monopoly favoring elite business interests and ignoring common laborers, especially farmers. He was further concerned that foreign interests owned 20 percent of the bank's stock. A man ruled by passion and conviction, Jackson became the first President to take direct action against the institution.

In 1832, Jackson vetoed legislation rechartering the National Bank, vowing to destroy "the monster." In September 1833, Jackson ordered Secretary of the Treasury William J. Duane to transfer federal funds from the National Bank to several state financial institutions. When Duane failed to comply with the President's directive, Jackson promptly fired him. The President immediately appointed Attorney General Roger Taney to serve as interim Secretary of Treasury. A loyal Jacksonian, Taney promptly carried out the President's transfer order.

Jackson's Whig opponents accused him of depositing federal funds in so-called "pet banks." Nicholas Biddle, President of the National

Bank, angrily reacted to the President's action by tightening credit and recalling loans, negatively impacting the American economy. Concerned citizens from around the country, fearful of a looming economic crisis, traveled to the White House in droves.

"Go see Nicholas Biddle," Jackson tersely informed visitors.

Jackson's financial decisions likely played a role in the Panic of 1937 inherited by his successor, Martin Van Buren. Kentucky Senator Henry Clay, a sworn enemy of Jackson, convinced most of his colleagues to formally censure the ex-President for terminating the National Bank. The House of Representatives, however, adopted a much different stance. Congressmen not only passed a resolution supporting Jackson's executive order but also proposed launching an investigation of potential financial irregularities involving the former National Bank.

Clay managed to exact a measure of revenge against Jackson by orchestrating the Senate's rejection of Roger Taney's permanent appointment as Secretary of the Treasury, the first time in history a Presidential appointment had been voted down by the legislative body. Jackson nonetheless considered his death blow to the National Bank a much-needed decentralization of power. On January 8, 1835, the lame duck President proudly announced the U.S. government had paid off its national debt for the first time in history.

Whig Party lawmakers found additional faults with Jackson in addition to his elimination of the National Bank. They accused him of unilaterally ignoring U.S. Supreme Court rulings. Whigs believed the Executive Branch of government had been transformed into an autocracy during Jackson's two terms as President.

While never an established anti-slavery party, many Whigs were confirmed Abolitionists. In sharp contrast, most all Southern Jacksonian Democrats as well as some Northern party members were pro-slavery. Jackson himself owned more than 150 slaves.

As the 1840 General Election approached, Whigs were primed to unseat the incumbent Democratic President. Party operatives focused on Martin Van Buren's perceived lack of financial acumen which resulted in the 1837 economic crisis.

Whig campaign ads lampooned the incumbent: "VAN, VAN IS A USED UP MAN and MARTIN VAN RUIN."

The Whigs also disingenuously portrayed Van Buren as a wealthy aristocrat while depicting William Henry Harrison as a commoner. Campaign literature pictured Harrison sipping cider outside a log cabin. Factually, Harrison was born to wealthy parents in a Virginia mansion, while Van Buren, the son of a tavern-keeper, was truly a self-made man.

Whig Party operatives also developed a long-remembered campaign slogan, reminding voters their candidate was a battlefield hero: "TIPPECANOE AND TYLER, TOO."

On Election Day 1840, approximately 80 percent of registered voters cast their ballots. Harrison defeated Van Buren by more than a million popular votes and dominated the Electoral College, 234-60. In addition, the Whig Presidential candidate carried 18 of 27 states.

(Van Buren would attempt to return to power four years later but failed to win the Democratic Party nomination. In 1848, he ran for President under the banner of the newly created, short-lived Free Soil Party. Finishing a distant third, Van Buren failed to win a single electoral vote. The former President soon retired to Lindewald, New York, not far from his birth place of Kinderhook. Van Buren died on July 24, 1862).

King was disheartened by 1840 election results. For the first time in history, Whigs won majorities in both houses of Congress. While King was re-elected to the Senate, he had faced stiff competition from John Gayle, his home state Whig Party opponent. Among all the Democratic lawmakers living in the same boarding house, only King and Buchanan retained their Congressional seats.

JACKSONIAN DEMOCRAT

On April 4, 1841, barely a month after delivering the longest Presidential inaugural address to date, President William Henry Harrison died of pneumonia. (His grandson, Benjamin Harrison, would be elected the 23rd President of the United States in 1888. This remains the first and only time in American history a grandfather and grandson have served as President).

Vice-President John Tyler ascended to the Presidency after Harrison's death. At this point in history, no provision existed for filling the vacant Vice-Presidential seat. (The 25th Amendment was ratified on *February 10, 1967*. The new amendment mandated the President nominate a Vice-President "who shall take office upon confirmation by a majority vote of both Houses of Congress." To date, the 25th Amendment has twice been invoked: Richard Nixon selected Gerald Ford to replace Vice-President Spiro Agnew after the latter resigned because of bribery and corruption charges and Ford [who ascended to the Presidency after Nixon himself resigned due to involvement in the Watergate scandal] selected Nelson Rockefeller to serve as his Vice-President).

As President Pro Tempore of the Senate, King was suddenly next in line to become President if Tyler died, became incapacitated, was impeached by the House and convicted by the Senate, or resigned. Harrison's death marked the first of three times King would find himself a heartbeat away from the Presidency.

President Tyler, a Virginia-born aristocrat, came from a family of slave holders. Originally a Democrat, Tyler joined the Whig Party after breaking with Andrew Jackson over the South Carolina tariff nullification crisis.

Leading Whig lawmakers, including Henry Clay, expected Tyler would loyally support all party policies. When the independent-minded former Democrat failed to strictly toe the party line, many Whigs derisively referred to the new President as "His Accidency."

Before his death, President Harrison had called for a special session of Congress to convene in the summer of 1841. Democratic Senators and Congressmen anticipated great difficulty preventing the Whig majority from implementing policies favoring a more powerful central government.

"The time is coming when we shall require our ablest men to guard our rights and protect our interests against federal encroachment," King wrote to Alabama Governor Arthur Bagby.

Democratic Senators and Congressman indeed mounted strong opposition to Whig proposals. In the end, Whig lawmakers failed to charter a new National Bank, fund all proposed government infrastructure projects, or significantly increase protective tariffs. More than once, Democrats were aided by President Tyler's veto of Whig-enacted bills.

While Whigs were in power, many Congressional Democrats limited their extracurricular activities. King uncharacteristically shunned most Washington, D.C. social functions.

"I have lived the quiet life of a Hermit this winter and can give you no account of the fashion and gaiety of Washington. But as I understand it had differed not at all from the past, abounding in mustached gentlemen without brains, and silly girls with whom they waltz," King caustically wrote his niece, Catherine Margaret Ellis.

As King and Buchanan spent more time together in the confines of shared boarding houses, their personal and political bonds strengthened. By this point in time, the Pennsylvania Senator was regarded as an unabashed "doughface"—a malleable man whose principles failed to align with the majority of citizens residing in his region of the country. More specifically, Buchanan was a Northern politician who clearly favored Southern interests.

From the beginning of his political career, Buchanan preferred the company of Southern lawmakers. He identified with their gentility, chivalry, and manner of social discourse. Even though he was Northern-born and professed personal hatred of slavery, Buchanan ardently defended the rights of slaveholders and played a key role in passing the Congressional "gag rule."

JACKSONIAN DEMOCRAT

In January 1836, Ohio Senator Thomas Morris, a member of the newly formed Whig Party, had introduced a pair of anti-slavery petitions on the legislative floor. Southern lawmakers, however, were primed to block formal debates concerning slavery. South Carolina Democratic Congressman James Henry Hammond successfully introduced a proposal banning open House floor discussions of resolutions concerning abolition of slavery or restrictions preventing spread of the "peculiar institution" into developing territories. In the Senate, John C. Calhoun mimicked the actions of his fellow South Carolinian. Dough-faced Senator Buchanan was among the lawmakers actively lobbying in favor of the Southern-born gag rule.

While he may have genuinely abhorred slavery, Buchanan detested Abolitionists far more, describing them as "fanatics." His logic, however, was based on perception rather than supporting evidence. Buchanan strongly believed the Abolitionist Movement was not "benefitting the slaves who are the objects of their regard," and if given the choice, would "have inflicted serious injuries upon them."

Buchanan also made the mistake of lumping all who opposed slavery into a single category. Abolitionists wanted the institution of slavery immediately and permanently revoked. Many others who opposed slavery did not call for abolishment, merely content with keeping involuntary servitude from spreading beyond existing borders. Some who favored ending slavery were by no means interested in promoting full citizenship for Blacks. Instead, they wanted all freed slaves to be colonized outside of the United States. Buchanan, however, stubbornly regarded all who opposed slavery as Abolitionists.

At the conclusion of debates between pro- and anti-slavery Senators, Buchanan pushed forward a resolution to "receive and reject" any motions deleterious to the institution of slavery. After the majority of Senators concurred with Calhoun and Buchanan, the gag rule remained in effect for 14 years.

Not surprisingly, King wholeheartedly supported his close friend's proposal. Taking leave from the President Pro Tempore's seat, King roamed the Senate gallery, actively encouraging colleagues to vote in favor of Buchanan's measure.

As a slave owner, King believed involuntary servitude was protected by the U.S. Constitution. Like many Southern plantation owners, King boldly declared slaves were not only happy with their work and living conditions but also received special care from their masters. The first assertion had no basis in fact. Secondly, not all slaveholders provided humane care, much less offered respect, to their human chattel.

Like Buchanan, King viewed Abolitionists as meddlesome and self-righteous. Accordingly, he voted to defeat an 1837 proposal banning slavery in the District of Columbia.

Dough-faced Buchanan went even further when defending slaveholders: "I might repeat here what I have said upon a former occasion: that all Christendom is leagued against the South upon this domestic issue of slavery. They have no allies to sustain their Constitutional rights, except the Democracy of the North."

As the 1844 election year approached, many politicos believed former President Martin Van Buren would win re-election and return a Democrat to the White House. In December 1843, however, Van Buren was victimized by a self-inflicted political wound. Fearing war with Mexico, he publicly spoke out against annexation of the newly established Republic of Texas. The ill-timed pronouncement alienated Van Buren from pro-slavery, expansionist-minded Southern Democrats and effectively doomed his chances of winning the Presidential nomination. In the wake of Van Buren's sincere but self-destructive pronouncement, other Democrats emerged as Presidential front runners, including Senator Lewis Cass of Michigan, Rear Admiral Charles Stewart of New Jersey, former Vice-President Richard Johnson, and Senator Levi Woodbury of New Jersey.

Delaying his own Presidential aspirations, James Buchanan was a Van Buren supporter. By remaining loyal to the former President,

Buchanan believed he would emerge as Democratic frontrunner in the 1848 Presidential election.

Entertaining an ulterior motive, King tried to persuade his friend to reconsider. If Buchanan won the Presidential nomination, King envisioned himself as an ideal running mate. King's strategy was not without merit. The ever-growing sectional conflict over slavery convinced the Democratic Party that it must field a ticket with candidates from the North and South. Buchanan for President and King for Vice-President would have achieved such balance.

King had long considered his roommate to be worthy of the Presidency, as Buchanan echoed in a letter to a friend: "Colonel King assures me that the Legislature of Alabama were [sic] anxious to nominate me, but he thought it indiscrete at the moment."

In the weeks and months leading up to the May 1844 Democratic National Convention, King was vocal in supporting Buchanan for President. King informed a fellow Alabama delegate that the Pennsylvania Senator was an "able and safe" candidate. Buchanan, however, appeared unwilling to reconsider a Presidential run.

While Buchanan waffled, King openly expressed interest in the Vice-Presidency. Interestingly, King never openly expressed interest in the Presidency. Perhaps he believed his abilities were better suited for the number two position, spanning both the Executive and Legislative branches of federal government. And if elected Vice-President in 1844, King would be well-positioned to help Buchanan capture the ultimate prize four years later.

King had at least one influential supporter in 1844. Early in the year, Francis Blair, editor of Washington, D.C.'s pro-Democratic newspaper, *The Daily Globe*, published an open letter published by Alabama Congressman William Winter Payne. Employing the pseudonym "Amicus," Payne opined King was the most deserving Democratic Vice-Presidential candidate based on "seniority" and "length of service."

Buchanan, perpetually indecisive and perhaps jealous at the prospect of his close friend's potential election to Executive office ahead of him, was hardly enthusiastic. While urging home state Democrats to support King's pursuit of the Vice-Presidency, Buchanan declined a fellow party member's request to compose King's campaign biography.

"Intimate as I am with Colonel King, I do not possess the necessary information to write a sketch of his public life, "Buchanan tartly replied.

Meanwhile, Tennessee State Democratic Party delegates heavily favored Governor James K. Polk, former Speaker of the U.S. House of Representatives, for Vice-President, or even the Presidency itself. In late 1843, presumably after Van Buren sabotaged his own Presidential bid by speaking out against the annexation of Texas, Andrew Jackson wrote his former Vice-President. The influential former President informed Van Buren that Polk was "the strongest and truest man in the South." As a rising star, Polk had already earned the nickname "Young Hickory," reminding voters of his iconic fellow Tennessean.

Tennessee Congressman Aaron Venable Brown, who equally detested King and Buchanan, published his own open letter in *The Daily Globe*. Adopting the rather conspicuous alias, "A Tennessee Democrat," he took direct aim at King by urging fellow Democrats to "abandon that system of puffing, blowing, and swelling, by which a toad may be magnified into the dimension of an ox."

Genteel and compromising by nature, King never publicly counterattacked Brown. However, he was not above aiming barbs at selected enemies during private conversations. He characterized John Quincy Adams as a "black-hearted old witch" and James K. Polk as a "very inferior man." Not yet done, King quietly opined Martin Van Buren was an "intriguing, selfish" politician.

King's bid for the Vice-Presidency in 1844 was ended by fate rather than convention politics. On February 28 of that year, President Tyler, Secretary of State Abel Upshur, Secretary of the Navy Thomas Gilmore, and a handful of other dignitaries were cruising the Potomac River aboard the warship *U.S.S. Princeton*. Suddenly and without warning, one of the vessel's cannons exploded. Six people were killed in the blast, including Upshur and Gilmore.

In the aftermath of this unforeseen tragedy, King was destined to pursue a new chapter in his life of public service.

5

Bon Voyage

After the tragic explosion aboard the *U.S.S. Princeton*, President Tyler was forced find a replacement for his deceased Secretary of State. In addition, the position of American Minister to France was vacant. When the President tried to appoint Congressman Henry A. Wise to the diplomatic post in Paris, the Senate refused to confirm the outspoken and cantankerous Virginian. To maintain regional balance in his Administration, Tyler looked for another Southerner to appoint to the key position.

At the time, the United States was facing potential armed conflicts on separate fronts. The President desperately sought a skilled and experienced negotiator who could convince France not to join forces with England in opposing American initiatives.

South of the border, Mexico was threatening war over America's planned annexation of Texas. After considerable bloodshed, Texas had escaped Mexican rule and became an independent republic in 1836. Mexico, however, still claimed ownership of Texas and was fully prepared to wage war over the issue. American expansionists, no less defiant concerning Texas' ultimate fate, were eager to call the Mexican government's bluff.

Presidents Jackson and Van Buren had carefully side-stepped the annexation issue, border conflicts between Texas and Mexico, and unsettled indemnity claims filed by American citizens against the Mexican government. Both Presidents believed with the passage of time Texas would naturally become part of the United States, absent bloodshed.

President Tyler, a proponent of America's self-conceived, divine right to add to her territory, commonly referred to as Manifest Destiny, had no intention of delaying westward expansion. Tyler sent the 1844 Treaty of Annexation to the Senate, fully intent upon moving Texas closer to statehood. On June 18 of that year, the Senate voted 35-16 against ratification. Non-expansionist Whigs voted in near unanimous opposition, 27-1. All Northern Whigs cast dissenting votes, while 14 of 15 Southern contemporaries joined in opposition, placing party loyalty above sectional interests. Meanwhile, most Democratic Senators, including 10 of 11 Southerners, voted in favor of ratifying the treaty. While the issue of annexation remained yet unsettled, the relationship between the U.S. and Mexico grew more contentious.

The Oregon Territory, home to the future states of Oregon, Washington, Idaho, and parts of Montana and Wyoming, was yet another diplomatic hot spot. Great Britain, Canada's ruling nation, was averse to ceding territory to establish a permanent national border. Furthermore, the British government threatened war if American expansionists tried push the line of demarcation further north.

President Tyler and his key advisors believed the U.S. could defeat Great Britian and Mexico if war broke out in one or both disputed regions. But if France joined forces with England, a two-front engagement would be more formidable.

The President soon summoned Senator King, a man he "greatly esteemed," to the White House: "I need you to go to France as our Minister. We have to keep them out of the Mexico-Texas disagreement and the Oregon boundary dispute in the North."

Tyler was fully aware England was lobbying France to form a unified anti-American alliance. King's fluency in French and reputation as conciliator made him the man of the hour.

"It appears that England doesn't feel strong enough to face us on both fronts, and they need an ally. If we can keep France out of it, everything will go a lot smoother, and hopefully, without war," Tyler further explained.

King, who anticipated the reason for Tyler's summons prior to the actual meeting, wrote to a friend: "I don't really want that task. I'd like to see how the upcoming Presidential race plays out. I think I have a fairly decent chance to become Vice-President."

King was in a bind not of his own making. As a Southern planter and slave owner, he was fully aware annexation of Texas would add vast territory to the country. Texas' climate and soil conditions were also ideal for large-scale cotton cultivation, meaning the republic would more than likely be admitted to the Union as a slave state.

On April 12, 1844, John C. Calhoun, newly appointed Secretary of State, officially informed King that President Tyler had appointed him Minister to France. The Senate quickly and unanimously confirmed his appointment. Three days later, King resigned from the Senate. (Alabama Governor Henry W. Collier appointed Benjamin Fitzpatrick as King's interim replacement).

King privately communicated disappointment about leaving the Senate, particularly relinquishing his role as President Pro Tempore. Discreet when sharing his true feelings, King wrote Governor Collier that he "yielded to the opinion and advice of friends on whom I rely, and not from any desire of office on my part."

"I am free to say that it was with this hope alone that I consented to abandon a more honorable situation—one every way congenial to my feelings—and for a season to place myself far distant from my home, my country, and friends," King continued in his missive to Collier.

While King gave every indication that he preferred to remain in the Senate, it is also possible the ambitious Alabamian realized short-term sacrifice might later prove advantageous. Serving as French Foreign Minister would be an impressive addition to the political resume of any politician coveting higher office, including the Vice-Presidency.

BON VOYAGE

After a brief trip to Alabama to settle personal affairs, King traveled to New York City, launch point for his journey to France. While in the Big Apple, King lodged with former Democratic Congressman James J. Roosevelt and his wife Cornelia Van Ness Roosevelt. (Cornelia was the daughter of Vermont Governor Cornelius Van Ness, who had served as a Foreign Minister during President Andrew Jackson's Administration. James J. Roosevelt was the paternal grandfather of future President Theodore Roosevelt). James and Cornelia were close friends to both King and James Buchanan.

During his brief stay in New York City, King wrote Buchanan apologizing for failing to personally bid him adieu. King explained that he wanted to "avoid the pain of saying good-bye."

In the same missive, King's tone was glum: "For myself, I shall feel lonely in the midst of Paris, for there I shall have no friends with whom I can commune my own thoughts."

On May 16, 1844, King boarded a trans-Atlantic steamship, *The Silvia de Grasse*. Twenty-eight-year-old Catherine Margaret Ellis, 26-year-old Alfred J. Beck, and 10-year-old William Thomas King joined their uncle on the voyage to France. The travel group also included John Bell, King's slave and newly designated valet.

Soon after arriving in Paris, King discovered his $9,000 annual salary was barely enough to cover rent on his palatial residence at 100 Rue Street Domingue. An affluent King, however, was capable of privately funding an entertainment and lifestyle budget befitting a Foreign Minister.

Catherine Margaret grew even closer to her uncle during their stay in France. Widowed since the unexpected death of her husband two years earlier, Catherine Margaret was grateful to travel outside the United States for the first time. For the remainder of her uncle's life, she would serve as his personal hostess and frequent travel companion.

Behaving more like daughter than niece, Catherine Margaret

boldly encouraged her uncle to seek a wife. King pleasantly replied that he was an "old bachelor" and "portended little prospect of giving you an aunt very shortly."

At age 58, King remained strikingly handsome with a refined yet pleasant demeanor. In addition to his official duties, the Foreign Minister was an active participant in Parisian social circles. Catherine Margaret was not the only relative who eventually concluded King's bachelorhood was by *choice* rather than *fate*.

"The old man is looking exceedingly well, and when he is dressed in his new wig and new hat, I would stake him against any old card of his age, and perhaps you think his days of conquest are over, but I can tell you are very mistaken, for I assure you that there is a young lady here, who never sees him without having hysterics for an hour after he leaves her," nephew William wrote to his father.

William was nonetheless realistic in his missive: "I fear he will never add to the number of the family, as he seems now satisfied to give away the young brides and stand Godfather to his young countrymen."

At least one individual outside the family hoped King would end his bachelorhood. South Carolina Democratic Senator Francis Pickens, one of King's former boarding house roommates, opined a "French lady" would be an ideal mate for the Foreign Minister.

On July 1, 1844, King presented his credentials to the French Court of St. Cloud. The American Foreign Minister hoped to establish a friendly and productive relationship with King Louise Philippe I to dissuade France from joining England attempting to block America's expansionist agenda.

Before King's first face-to-face meeting with Philippe at a formal dinner on July 4, the French monarch sent the American envoy an encouraging note: "Mr. King, I am not unacquainted with your eminence in the American Republic. I know with how much ability you have filled many posts of honor, and I am now really rejoiced that a man of so much experience and so much fame as a statesman represents that great republic of yours at this court."

By established protocol, messages from the American Foreign Minister were first passed through the French Foreign Office. King, however, convinced Philippe to accept direct correspondence without prior screening.

In the very beginning, Philippe proclaimed Texas should remain an independent republic. King's initial reply was tactful; if Texas joined the United States, new trade opportunities would benefit all of Europe. As negotiations progressed, King boldly proclaimed no foreign nations possessed sufficient influence or firepower to prevent the United States from annexing Texas and establishing a favorable northwest border with Canada. King further pointed out an alliance between the French and English governments would result in dissolution of friendly relations between France and the United States.

King Philippe was impressed by King's candor and rationale. Before long, the French monarch promised "no steps would be taken by this government hostile to the American government."

Ashbel Smith, official Envoy from the Republic of Texas, assured Phillipe that France's policy of non-intervention was just and wise. The ultimate decision, however, required approval from Francois Guizot, the French Minister of Foreign Affairs. With little fanfare, Guizot confirmed France *would not align with any European country* to block America's annexation of Texas. The American and Canadian border proved inconsequential to the French government, requiring little in the way of formal negotiations.

While his mission was a total success, King privately expressed self-doubt. He wrote Buchanan that his "hands trembled like an alarmed school boy before the dreaded pedagogue" during negotiations with French officials.

"My unfortunate delivery convinces me that I am not fitted for diplomacy, and causes me to regret still more, that I ever consented to accept of a situation for which I was so illy qualified," King further informed Buchanan.

Were King's self-deprecatory remarks genuine? Or was he merely planting a seed in his friend's head? If James K. Polk was elected President in the forthcoming election, Buchanan was considered a leading choice to become Secretary of State. If those events transpired, Buchanan might well convince Polk to recall King from France at the earliest possible date.

While eagerly awaiting an opportunity to return home, King kept a distant eye on American politics. Not surprisingly, he was most interested in the Democratic Party's Presidential and Vice-Presidential candidates.

When the 1844 Democratic National Convention convened at the Egyptian Saloon of the Old Fellows Hall in Baltimore, former President Martin Van Buren won the most votes on the first ballot but failed to secure a 2/3rd majority. Over the course of several subsequent ballots, Michigan Senator Lewis Cass surpassed Van Buren's delegate count but was also unable to win the requisite majority.

James K. Polk, the 9th Governor of Tennessee and former U.S. Speaker of the House, entered the convention as a presumptive Vice-Presidential candidate. As balloting for top spot on the ticket remained in a stalemate, Polk's political operatives spread word among delegates that Polk was iconic Andrew Jackson's *first choice* to become the next *President*.

After eight deadlocked ballots, Van Buren's home state delegation removed his name from consideration. On the 9th ballot, Polk became the first "dark horse" major political party nominee in American history. News of Polk's unexpected candidacy was relayed from Baltimore to Washington, D.C. as the inaugural message transmitted by a revolutionary communication system, Samuel F. B. Morse's telegraph machine.

Convention delegates then selected George Mifflin Dallas, a Pennsylvania lawyer, former U.S. Senator, and one-time Foreign Minister to Russia and Great Britain, for Vice-President. James Buchanan was insulted when a *fellow Pennsylvanian* was nominated for national office ahead of him. (The origins of the name Dallas, Texas have long been a subject of debate. Many historians believe the city was named in honor of George Mifflin Dallas by the community's founder, John Neely Bryan, who was a close friend of the Pennsylvanian. Others believe only Dallas County bears Polk's running mate's last name, and the city itself took the name of Trevanion B. Dallas, a local lawyer and judge.)

King expressed displeasure with the actions of Democratic convention delegates. In a private letter to Buchanan, he denounced Polk and Dallas as "bad selections" to head the party ticket. King also predicted the Whig Party candidate would win the November General Election. Despite his sense of betrayal, Buchanan remained a loyal Democrat and campaigned on behalf of the Polk/Dallas Presidential ticket in Pennsylvania and Ohio.

Incumbent President John Tyler, having been expelled by the Whigs for repeatedly vetoing the party's legislative proposals, was nominated by the temporarily revived, Jefferson-Era Democratic- Republican Party on May 27, 1844. Fearing the resurrected party would attract traditional Democratic votes, Polk arranged for a private meeting with Tyler. If elected President, Polk promised he would support ratification of a new Texas annexation treaty, one of Tyler's great disappointments during his Presidency. On August 20, after receiving Polk's reassurance, the incumbent President ended his third- party bid.

In May of that year, Whig Party stalwart Henry Clay was nominated to run for President a *third* time. Clay was already on record opposing annexation of Texas, fearing Mexico would declare war against the United States. While opposition to annexation would prove unpopular in many circles, particularly the South, most Whigs believed the Great Compromiser represented their best chance to capture the Presidency.

Whig delegates nominated New Jersey U.S. Senator Theodore

Frelinghuysen as Clay's running mate. Nicknamed the "Christian Statesman," Frelinghuysen was perhaps best known for advocating colonization of slaves rather than abolition, making him an acceptable choice among Southern Whigs.

Whigs soon adopted the party's official campaign slogan: "HURRAY, HURRAY, THE COUNTRY'S RISIN'—VOTE FOR CLAY AND FRELINGHYSEN."

Whig political operatives were acutely aware opposition to annexation of Texas would alienate many Southern voters. Consequently, the party platform focused almost exclusively on improvements in America's infrastructure and sound economic policies.

In sharp contrast, the Democratic platform was provocative: "REANNEXATION FOR TEXAS AND OREGON and 54-40 OR FIGHT." (The latter referenced the proposed latitudinal demarcation for a permanent Canadian border).

The 1844 Presidential Election result were the closest in 20 years:

	POLK	**CLAY**
Popular votes:	1,339,494	1,300,005
Electoral vote:	170	105
Popular vote percentage:	49.5	48.1
States won:	15	11

Voters south of the Mason-Dixon Line played an instrumental role in determining the outcome of the election. Excepting Virginia, Polk swept the South.

Still residing in France, King did not learn about the election results for several days. While delighted by the Democratic triumph, King had significant concerns about the President-Elect. Would annexation of Texas and the Canadian border issue be too complex for Polk to handle? King believed Polk was underqualified to serve as Vice-President, much less Commander-in-Chief.

King shared his concerns about the President-Elect in a letter to Buchanan: "Were he a man of great firmness of character, which I fear he is not, and would take helm of state into his own hands, he probably would be able to steer clear of the breakers by which he will be surrounded, but if he wavers, he is lost and the party with him."

King's outlook brightened after Polk appointed Buchanan Secretary of State. King was confident his friend would provide the new President a wise and steady hand when dealing with annexation of Texas and negotiation of a permanent border between the Oregon Territory and Canada.

King nonetheless wrote Buchanan that he longed to turn back the hands of time: "Most sincerely do I wish that we both remained in the Senate."

While the new Secretary of State played an instrumental role in settling the Canadian border issue without provoking war against England, President Polk grew frustrated with Buchanan's perpetual indecisiveness and eccentric behaviors. When Buchanan expressed interest in a vacancy on the U.S. Supreme Court, Polk seized upon an opportunity to remove the fickle Secretary of State from his Cabinet.

Buchanan, however, delayed accepting appointment to the high court, believing he, alone, would be allowed to handpick his Cabinet successor. The President was irked by Buchanan's sense of entitlement and plan to select King as the next Secretary of State.

In February 1846, King wrote Buchanan professing disinterest in the Cabinet post: "I feel but too sensibly my inability, properly to discharge the duties of so important a station, to attribute the suggestion to anything else than personal regard of yourself."

Eager to return home from France, King soon changed his mind about Buchanan's proposal. Normally discrete, King made it known his appointment as Secretary of State was a done deal.

Polk, however, planned to name Louis McLane, current American Minister to England, former Delaware U.S. Congressman and Senator, and prior Secretary of State and the Treasury during Andrew Jackson's Administration, as Buchanan's replacement. McLane soon notified the

President that King was informing others of his forthcoming appointment as Secretary of State. Angered by Buchanan's presumptuousness and King indiscretion, Polk wrote McLane and assured him King was not under consideration for *any* Cabinet post. Polk's declaration quickly brought an end to Buchanan's grandiose scheme to personally choose his successor.

All the while, Buchanan struggled to make up his mind about the President's offer to appoint him to the Supreme Court. His main concern was no active or former Supreme Court Justice had ever been elected President of the United States. Despite the prestige of serving on the high court, Buchanan feared forfeiting his Presidential dreams. From his post in Paris, King was definitely opposed to his friend accepting the Supreme Court appointment.

"Retain your place, regardless of minor annoyances," King advised Buchanan.

In another sharply worded missive, he advised Buchanan "to abandon all idea of the Judgeship." King further predicted that if Buchanan remained Secretary of State, he would "find the field open for the Presidency, unless you place yourself on the shelf by the Judgeship."

When King heard rumors that Buchanan might also be interested in becoming America's Foreign Minister to England, his reaction was decidedly different. Unlike the Supreme Court, King considered diplomatic posts as ideal launch pads for Presidential aspirants.

"If I were certain you would come to England, I should be almost reconciled to remain another year in France, as few hours suffices for passing from Paris to London, and we could visit each other frequently without detriment to the public service," King enthusiastically wrote his friend.

It is uncertain if Buchanan was truly interested in serving as Foreign Minister to England. His interest in the Supreme Court vacancy was also waning. At the 11th hour, Buchanan informed the President that wished to remain Secretary of State.

In 1844, Congress officially approved annexation of the Republic of Texas. On December 29, 1845, Texas was admitted as the 28th state to the Union. A staunch advocate of Manifest Destiny, President Polk was eager to acquire the New Mexico and California Territories from Mexico. After Mexico refused to sell those lands, Polk was poised to seize them by force.

Secretary of State Buchanan cautiously advised the President to wait until Mexico instigated hostilities before declaring war. Polk, however, was beyond restraint. In February 1847, the President ordered U.S. Army General Zachary Taylor to cross the Nueces River and set up camp in disputed territory just north of the Rio Grande River.

Reacting to deliberate provocation, Mexican troops began skirmishing with their American counterparts. The so-called Thornton Affair, named for Captain Seth Thornton whose troops were ambushed by Mexican soldiers, precipitated yet another conflict, the Battle of Alto. On May 13, 1847, at the President's urging, Congress voted to declare war against Mexico.

Meanwhile, King was more than eager to return home. Having successfully convinced France not to interfere with American expansionism, King was not only homesick but also complained Paris' climate aggravated his age-induced rheumatism.

In June 1846, King submitted a written request to President Polk asking to be recalled from his overseas diplomatic post: "My private affairs renders [sic] it of utmost importance for me to visit Alabama, even if it were a leave of absence."

Secretary of State Buchanan soon informed King that Polk had accepted his resignation. At the same time, Buchanan assured his close friend the President would have been "most happy had you consented to remain." The Secretary of State was delighted when Polk accepted his recommendation and appointed Richard Rush, American Minister to England during the Administrations of Presidents James Monroe and John Quincy Adams, as King's replacement.

According to his niece and nephews, King was generous until the very end of his stay in France. Before departing Paris, King *gave* his carriage and horses to Francois, the Foreign Minister's loyal coachman.

During the return voyage to America, King and his travel companions encountered peril. In late September 1846, the group boarded a steamship, *The Great Britain*, launched from Liverpool, England and bound for New York City. Early in the voyage, the vessel crashed into a rocky reef off the coast of Ireland.

Immediately after the jarring collision, King knocked on his niece's stateroom door: "Come out as soon as you can, for we will soon be in eternity. The boat is grounded and will soon go to pieces."

The Great Britain's passengers, crew, and captain were fortunate enough to evacuate the sinking vessel aboard lifeboats. After safely returning to terra firma, a fellow passenger recalled King was grateful to be in Ireland, "the site of the Battle of the Boyne, the place where my ancestor fought for the Prince of Orange." (On July 1, 1690, during the Battle of the Boyne, forces loyal to sitting Protestant King William III and his wife Queen Mary II waged war against newly recruited and mostly untrained soldiers supporting deposed Catholic monarch, King James II. Prior to being crowned King of England in 1689, William III had lived in the Netherlands bearing the title of Prince William of Orange. The Battle of the Boyne was fought near the town of Drogheda in what was then known as the Kingdom of Ireland. After William III's army quickly triumphed, James II fled to France and never returned home. Out of 50,000 participants, nearly 2,000 died during the conflict).

After remaining in Ireland for a few weeks before booking safe passage aboard a packet ship, King finally headed back to America, eager to pursue his political ambitions.

6

Aunt Fancy and Miss Nancy

The most controversial and speculative aspects of William R. King's life center around his sexual orientation, and more specifically, the exact nature of his relationship with fellow statesman James Buchanan. Were the pair merely close friends or closeted same sex lovers? While speculation and fact occasionally intersect, divergence remains equally likely.

The allegations that both men were gay took root while they were serving together in the U.S. Senate. Several of their contemporaries, more often than not motivated by personal and/or political animosities, accused King and Buchanan of engaging in "unnatural acts."

Whether their relationship was platonic or sexual in nature, King and Buchanan no doubt shared a close bond for nearly two decades leading up to King's death in 1853. Beginning in 1834, the pair roomed together for 10 years at various Washington, D.C. boarding houses, most often accompanied by a small, varying cast of fellow lawmakers.

Lifelong bachelors, King and Buchanan hosted and attended various social functions in a manner akin to husband and wife. They also exchanged private written correspondence, a portion of which has been lost to history. Some researchers claim the most intimate and revealing of those letters were later destroyed by their respective nieces to protect their uncles' reputations. (Those allegations will be explored in greater detail in the Afterword section of this narrative).

⁓⁓⁓

Joint habitation by lawmakers during the early- to mid-19th Century was common. Lack of available housing in the District of Columbia forced many government officials to share living spaces. Furthermore, less affluent lawmakers could not afford to rent, much less purchase and maintain a second residence, for occupation only during Congressional sessions. Consequently, many Congressman and Senators, both single and married, lived together in boarding houses, commonly referred to as "messes."

For approximately $10 per week, lawmakers could lease sparsely furnished single rooms containing a bed, dresser, and nightstand. Those who were accompanied by family members during Congressional sessions often rented suites of rooms.

While meals were included in monthly rent, boarders who regularly consumed alcohol were required to purchase their own spirits. After dinner, messmates often gathered in common areas for fellowship. Amid clouds of cigar and pipe smoke, discussions often centered around so-called "parlor politics."

At this point in history, Congressman and Senators had not yet been afforded dedicated work spaces, and boarding house rooms also functioned as de facto offices. (The now familiar House and Senate office buildings flanking Capitol Hill's main dome-topped structure were not constructed until the early 20th Century).

Messes usually consisted of lawmakers sharing common political philosophies. While King and Buchanan lived under the same roof for nearly a decade, fellow messmates often changed at the beginning of new Congressional sessions. On occasion, King and Buchanan *may* have been the only two lawmakers occupying the same boarding house. Democratic lawmakers Robert Carter Nicholas of Louisiana, Bedford Brown of North Carolina, Edward Lucas of Virginia, John Pendleton

King of Georgia, and William Henry Roane of Virginia were among their roommates.

Messes were generally limited to men only. In November 1841, however, King and Buchanan occupied a boarding house on C Street owned by a Mrs. Dashiell. During that Congressional term, Associate Supreme Court Justice John Catron and his *wife* Matilda were fellow messmates. For the most part, King and Buchanan joined a small, revolving cast of *men* fraternally occupying the same residence.

✿

Bachelorhood alone has never been a reliable predictor of sexual orientation. In the 1830s, the national average for unwedded men, including single, divorced, or widowed, was estimated at three percent. Among Congressmen and Senators, the figure was closer to *seven percent*.

Nonetheless, many prominent political figures ridiculed King and Buchanan. Crusty Andrew Jackson regularly poked fun at their so-called "friendship," nicknaming Buchanan "Aunt Fancy" and King "Miss Nancy."

Aaron Venable Brown, one-time Governor of Tennessee, U.S. Congressman, and Postmaster General of the United States, snidely referred to the messmates as "Buchanan and his wife." Of note, Brown and King were long-time bitter personal and political enemies.

Caustic barbs were not restricted by gender. President John Tyler's wife likened King and Buchanan to "Siamese twins," referencing the famous conjoined twins, Chang and Eng Butler.

Chang and Eng were born on May 11, 1811, in a Siam fishing village, present day Thailand. The sons of a Chinese father and half-Chinese, half-Malaysian mother, their birth country gave rise to the now familiar term Siamese twins. Joined at the waist by a tubular-shaped band of tissue, 3.25-inches-long and 1.5-inches wide, Chang and Eng shared a common umbilical cord and experienced simultaneous and identical bodily sensations throughout their lives.

The twins eventually adopted the surname, Bunker. In 1829, Chang and Eng moved to the United States. After conducting thorough physical examinations, a team of American physicians concluded both men would die if surgically separated.

The conjoined twins adapted remarkably well to their condition. In addition to running, swimming, and performing acrobatics, both were excellent marksmen. Chang and Eng soon began touring the United States and England performing acrobatic stunts and delivering lectures in front of large audiences Early on, the twins' stage performances were managed by agents, including legendary circus promoter P. T. Barnum. Concerned about financial exploitation by shady managers, Chang and Eng eventually took exclusive control of their traveling exhibitions.

In 1839, having accumulated considerable savings from a decade of public performances, the twins settled in Mount Airy, North Carolina. Fluent in English, they worked for a time as merchants before purchasing 200 acres in Surry County. Chang and Eng subsequently became prosperous, slaveholding tobacco planters.

In 1843, the twins married sisters, Adelaide and Sarah Yate. At first, all four slept together in a single bed. Chang and Eng eventually purchased separate residences, a mile and a half apart, and alternated between houses every fourth day. Collectively, the brothers fathered 21 children. Each had a son who later fought for the Confederacy during the Civil War.

By the end of the Civil War, the twins had lost considerable money as well as a combined 18 slaves. In 1869, the financially strapped brothers resumed touring exhibitions.

Though physically attached for their lifetime, the twins developed unique personalities and personal interests. Chang, more dominant and outspoken, enjoyed hunting and playing cards. He was also prone to self-medicating his mood swings with alcohol. Quieter and more reserved, Eng preferred to read and play chess.

On January 17, 1874, at the age of 62, Chang died suddenly after suffering a stroke. Three hours later, Eng expired. The exact cause of Eng's death was never officially documented, but at least one physician speculated he was literally "scared to death" by remaining physically attached to "a dead man."

In Philadelphia, an autopsy was performed to learn more about conjoined twins' anatomy and physiology. Dissection and analysis revealed Chang and Eng shared a fused liver but were otherwise anatomically normal. The Bunker brothers were buried at Mount Airy's White Plains Baptist Church.

Like certain politicians, newspaper reporters took pot shots at King and Buchanan, portraying their relationship in the most unfavorable light. In 1837, *The New York Herald* reported King was "an old bachelor, very prim in his appearance, and old maidish in his habits, and has, on that account, I presume, been called Miss Nancy—a cognomen which he still bears."

In 1844, prior to King's appointment as Foreign Minister to France, rumors about a gay relationship with Buchanan intensified. *The National Intelligencer*, a Washington D.C., Whig-controlled newspaper, described King and Buchanan as the "Orestes and Pylades of the Senate." (In Greek mythology, Orestes and Pylades were male friends and lovers).

In the widely read article, editor William Seaton added further fuel to the fire: "The only regret I have heard expressed is that two such long-tired and faithful friends as Messrs. Buchanan and King should be separated after a social and political union of so many years. Talk of the chords of love, the *vinculum matrimonii*, the loves of Jonathan and David, which passeth that of women—all is mere manner of moon shine compared to the regard which these two worthy bachelors entertain for one another."

The salacious and unsubstantiated barbs aimed at King and

THE 25-DAY VICE-PRESIDENT

Buchanan were not only motivated by personal animosity but also partisan politics. Whigs and Democrats frequently launched attacks at opposition party members. *The North American*, a Philadelphia-based, pro-Whig newspaper, declared King was Buchanan's "alter ego." Another anti-Democratic publication, *The Charleston Mercury*, referred to the messmates as "two princesses of bachelors."

Vice-Presidential biographer Sol Barzman later offered a salient observation. Barzman wrote that King's "fastidious habits and conspicuous intimacy with the bachelor Buchanan gave rise to cruel jibes."

While King and Buchanan no doubt shared many commonalities, there were notable differences in appearance, mannerisms, and behaviors. Though he was five years older than Buchanan, most observers regarded King as considerably more handsome. Six feet tall, with a trim physique, King was more statuesque than average men of his generation. His clean-shaven face, aquiline nose, and piercing eyes added to King's attractive countenance.

Despite a generous head of hair, King often concealed much of it beneath an outmoded powdered wig. While some observers described his mannerisms as effeminate, such characterizations were not universal. Many of King's friends and fellow lawmakers viewed him as quite masculine.

"Colonel King is about six feet high, remarkably erect in figure, and is well proportioned," one colleague noted, before adding, "Brave and chivalrous in his character, his whole bearing leaves even strangers with the conviction that they are in the presence of a finished gentleman."

While Buchanan was also six feet in height, his body shape was mesomorphic. Blond-haired with pale blue eyes, the Pennsylvanian possessed certain feminine characteristics, including a smooth complexion and long, slender fingers. Curiously, Buchanan was never able *to grow whiskers*, further separating him from conventional masculine stereotypes. (Some researchers have posited Buchanan's physical features were indicative of testosterone deficiency).

Buchanan also dressed differently than most men of his generation. His dark suits were offset by formal high stock collars. Shunning fashionable bow ties, Buchanan wore carefully knotted white kerchiefs that hung over his lapels.

When posing for photographs or engaged in one-on-one conversations, Buchanan cocked his head forward and slightly to the left. The odd posturing was a means of correcting his poor vision; Buchanan was far sighted in one eye and near sighted in the other.

By accepted standards, King was more masculine in appearance than his close friend. Buchanan's physical features, choice of attire, and odd mannerisms were particularly noticeable when in the presence of other men.

Neither King nor Buchanan were known to have publicly acknowledged rumors about their sexual orientation. King, however, was clearly bolder than Buchanan when his honor and integrity were affronted, even to the point of risking his own life.

In the spring of 1831, during Congressional recess, King returned home to Alabama. On the night of May 21, he encountered an area resident, Michael Johnson Kenan, on the streets of downtown Cahaba. The pair soon exchanged unpleasantries. The origin of the argument is open to speculation. Some observers recall Kenan berating King for actively campaigning on behalf of John Murphy, who was elected to the U.S. House of Representatives representing Alabama's 5th Congressional District. For reasons unknown, Kenan intensely disliked Murphy, a former two-term Governor and member of the state's North Carolina political faction. Others, however, remembered Kenan accusing King of purposefully blocking his appointment as Cahaba's Register of the Land Office.

As the altercation intensified, an intoxicated Kenan shoved King. The Alabama Senator reacted by wielding his sword cane—a walking stick with a concealed blade—and struck Kenan across his face with the blade's flat side. Aware Kenan was drunk, King's gesture was purely defensive.

"I thought you were a gentleman, but I see that was a mistake," King proclaimed, before withdrawing his weapon and exiting town on horseback.

The following morning, one of Kenan's friends, John C. Perry, visited King at his plantation home. Perry carried with him a letter written by Kenan challenging King to a duel.

King's immediate response was dismissive: "Mr. Perry, I don't consider him a gentleman, for he insulted me without cause. But I consider you a gentleman. If you had challenged me, I would have accepted it."

"Then I will take his place," Perry reflexively replied.

Likely caught off guard, King refused to back down. Since he had been challenged to a duel, King was permitted to select his weapon of choice. Still handy with a pistol, he was nonetheless concerned his eyesight had worsened with aging. Consequently, King opted for the broad sword, a weapon he could adeptly wield.

The proposed duel proved rather unusual, namely because King had been challenged by a man who was not directly involved in the precipitating altercation. By custom, each dueler was obligated to choose a "second." Designated backups were prepared to substitute if the duel participant became incapacitated prior to the face-off. In many cases, seconds wisely negotiated peaceful compromises, averting bloodshed.

King asked John Coffee, a Virginia-born, Alabama migrant and former U.S. Army General who fought under Andrew Jackson during both the Creek War and War of 1812, to serve as his second. (Coffee was also a renowned surveyor who had fixed the permanent border between Alabama and Mississippi. As an aside, the author's home county in southeast Alabama is named in honor of Coffee).

"The quarrel is entirely political, and I was very desirous to have for my friend one whose political integrity and firmness could not be questioned," King wrote Coffee.

Perry engaged William S. Taylor as his second. Taylor, a Georgia Faction loyalist and future commander of the Alabama State Militia, was noted for his bravery.

King selected August 8, 1831, as the date for the duel and opted for a location within the confines of northwest Alabama's Chickasaw Agency. King may have picked a distant killing field to draw less attention from home area residents. Furthermore, dueling was illegal in many parts of the country. When Aaron Burr killed Alexander Hamilton in June 1804, perhaps the most infamous duel in American history, the two combatants were obliged to exit New York by rowing across the Hudson River. Burr subsequently shot Hamilton to death in Weehawken, New Jersey, where violent displays of manhood and honor were still legal.

King's choice of weapons proved fortuitous. Perry, fully expecting the combatants would employ traditional dueling pistols, immediately grew fearful.

"I have never had a sword in my hand in my life. I don't wish to be murdered for any friendship for anyone," Perry protested.

His honor preserved, King agreed to cancel the duel. While he avoided committing a murder or suffering death, many men of his generation applauded King's show of bravado.

Ten years later, King was challenged to another duel. In early 1841, William Seaton, publisher of a pro-Whig newspaper, *The National Intelligencer*, and government print contract holder, wrote an article welcoming President-Elect William Henry Harrison to Washington, D.C. Offended by the newspaper's blatant political partisanship, King openly criticized Seaton as well as Joseph Gales, owner of the widely read publication.

Offended by King's remarks, Seaton challenged the Alabama Senator to a duel. Seaton recruited Whig Senator Willie P. Magnum of North Carolina to serve as his second. Even though he was a Whig Party member, South Carolina Senator William C. Preston volunteered to serve King in the same capacity.

According to Seaton, his opponent ultimately negotiated a peaceful resolution to their angry impasse: "Finally, Mr. King's better feeling asserted itself. He manfully and honorably avowed himself in the wrong, the result of spirited correspondence was made public, and the friendship between Mr. Seaton and himself, begun in early manhood, was renewed."

In March of that year, while Congress was still in session, King was challenged to a third duel. James Buchanan inadvertently set the wheels in motion by introducing a measure to eliminate the position of Senate Sergeant-at-Arms. Henry Clay, Kentucky Senator and Whig Party leader, openly opposed Buchanan's measure. In partisan political fashion, an angry Clay retaliated by proposing non-renewal of the Senate's printing contract with Francis Blair, editor of *The Washington Globe*, Democratic Party supporter and ardent defender of former President Andrew Jackson. In place of Blair, Clay proposed awarding the lucrative printing contract to a Whig loyalist. In partisan defiance, King publicly stated Blair's character compared "gloriously and proudly to Mr. Clay's."

Clay was clearly offended by King's declaration, as reflected in a letter written by Tennessee Senator Alfred Nicholson to President Polk: "Mr. Clay considered this remark as placing Blair on an equality with himself, and therefore pronounced it fake and cowardly."

Convinced his honor was at stake, Clay branded King a vengeful liar: "That is false. It is slanderous, base, and a cowardly declaration, and the Senator knows it not to be so."

Rather than confronting King in person, Clay sent his colleague from Alabama a letter challenging him to a duel. The hastily composed missive was hand delivered by Clay's proxy, Missouri Democratic Senator Lewis Fields Linn.

"I have no reply to make, none whatsoever. But Mr. Clay deserves a response," King informed Linn.

For unexplained reasons, King chose two seconds, Senator Linn and Ambrose Hundley Sevier, Democratic Senator from Arkansas. Meanwhile, Clay asked Virginia Senator William Archer to serve as his second.

While Clay's challenge was more likely symbolic than literal, King's close friend William Marcy, former Governor of New York, feared the worst: "King is a fighting man and I do not see how a duel can be honestly avoided unless Mr. C makes a retraction and unequivocal apology."

Before the situation got out of hand, Senate Sergeant-at-Arms Edward Dyer arrested both King and Clay and took them to appear before a local judge. As the challenger, Clay was forced to post $5,000 bond and promised the jurist he "would keep the peace, and particularly towards William R. King." After both men were released from custody, King insisted on an "unequivocal apology" from Clay.

On March 14, 1841, Clay formally issued a public apology for publicly airing his anger and resentment. King soon reciprocated.

Afterwards, Clay walked to King's desk on the Senate floor and asked for a "pinch of snuff." King not only honored the request but also rose from his seat and shook Clay's hand. The public reconciliation between two proud lawmakers precipitated "spontaneous applause from the gallery."

In the aftermath of an aborted conflict, John Forney, editorialist for *The Washington Daily Union,* offered his own assessment about the affair. He opined King was a "courtly gentleman as ever breathed." At the same time, Forney proclaimed the Alabamian "would have fought Mr. Clay without hesitation."

On three separate occasions, King readily accepted challenges to participate in potentially deadly conflicts after his honor and integrity were called into question. His willingness to engage an opponent using a broadsword or pistols was symbolic of 19th Century bravery. King's willingness to engage in armed conflict also contradicted existing biases about the manliness of gay individuals.

More than one of King's friends or colleagues described him as a "fighting man." Willing to risk life and limb in defense of honor, King displayed bravado alien to Buchanan. At most, Buchanan resorted to private verbal dissents when deflecting criticisms about his politics and integrity. For their time and place in history, King was regarded as more *manly* than Buchanan.

While more alike than not, King and Buchanan began their lives and political careers at opposite poles. Born in North Carolina and transplanted to Alabama, King was a lifelong Southerner. Early on, King identified as a Democratic-Republican before seamlessly evolving into a Jacksonian Democrat. As a man of the people, King consistently opposed high protective tariffs and wholeheartedly supported America's participation in the War of 1812.

Pennsylvania-born Buchanan was initially a member of the Federalist Party, cut from the same cloth as Founding Fathers John Adams and Alexander Hamilton, both of whom were considered aristocratic believers in a strong federal government. As a Federalist, Buchanan not only supported the National Bank and high protective tariffs but also opposed America's participation in the War of 1812. Consequently, his transformation to a Jacksonian Democrat was more dramatic than King's but consistent with Buchanan's lifelong propensity to change his mind about issues both large and small.

Even though King and Buchanan rarely canceled out each other's vote on the Senate floor, there were notable exceptions. While King repeatedly supported the federal government selling public lands to western settlers, Buchanan often opposed such measures. As a staunch fiscal conservative, King voted against federally funded pensions for Revolutionary War widows, purchase of additional books to stock the shelves of the Library of Congress, and governmental acquisition of President James Madison's personal papers, even when Buchanan supported those proposals. On larger issues of the day, however, King and Buchanan were most likely in agreement.

The bedrock of long-standing relationships includes trust, shared beliefs, similarities in personality, and mutual respect. Casting aside rumors about their sexual orientation, King and Buchanan shared more than enough commonalities to establish an enduring friendship.

Both could influence the other's personal and professional opinions. Dough-faced Buchanan readily adopted King's romanticized view of the Antebellum South. As a Union Loyalist, King often received more support and praise from Northern Democrats than his Southern colleagues.

AUNT FANCY AND MISS NANCY

Both King and Buchanan attributed past failed romantic relationships as impermeable roadblocks to future marriage. Each man confessed to familiarity with lost or unrequited love involving women.

In 1819, at age 28, Buchanan became engaged to 23-year-old Ann Coleman, daughter of a wealthy Pennsylvania iron mill owner. Buchanan had developed an earlier acquaintanceship with Ann's father, a fellow volunteer at Union Fire Company Number One. In addition, Buchanan attended St. James Episcopal Church, where the Coleman family were also communicants.

Buchanan's letters to Coleman suggested genuine love: "I pledge my all to you."

By late summer 1819, the couple's engagement was public knowledge in the Lancaster area. Rather than progressing to marriage, the relationship would end in tragedy.

In the weeks prior to setting an actual wedding date, Buchanan was busily engaged as the attorney representing the Columbia Bridge Company in a major lawsuit. The case consumed much of the young lawyer's time, as well as necessitating frequent trips from Lancaster to Pittsburgh.

Ann grew increasingly concerned her fiancée was devoting more energy and interest to his work than to nurturing their relationship. In November of that year, the conflict came to a head after Buchanan returned home from yet another sojourn to Pittsburgh. Rather than immediately visiting Ann, Buchanan stopped at the home of fellow attorney William Jenkins and his wife, Mary Field Hubley Jenkins. Grace Hubley, Mary's unmarried sister, was also present when Buchanan arrived. In the hour or so he remained at the Jenkins' house, Buchanan spent much of the time conversing with Grace.

Grace fueled flames of discontent by sending Ann Coleman a note detailing her enjoyable discourse with Buchanan. An enraged and jealous Ann soon dispatched a letter to her fiancée by courier, abruptly ending their engagement. Buchanan, who received the missive working in the courthouse, immediately turned pale. After recovering from initial shock, Buchanan cooly informed friends and family that Ann's decision to end their relationship was precipitated by a "trivial disagreement."

Even though she initiated the break, Ann was no less devastated and soon became distracted, withdrawn, and depressed. After a month passed, Mr. and Mrs. Coleman suggested their daughter travel to Philadelphia and visit with extended family, hoping time and distance would help mend her broken heart.

Ann's melancholia, however, failed to lift. After contracting a respiratory infection, she began ingesting laudanum, an alcohol and morphine solution easily obtainable and commonly ingested, often absent proper supervision, to treat a variety of maladies.

On the night of December 8, 1819, a physician was summoned after Ann's physical and mental well-being gravely worsened. Lacking evidence of an obvious physical malady, the doctor diagnosed her with "hysterical convulsions." Regardless of the underlying cause, Ann's condition rapidly deteriorated, and she was pronounced dead by daybreak. Family members and close friends believed the distraught young woman purposefully overdosed on laudanum, though suicide was never conclusively proven.

Several Lancaster residents directly blamed Buchanan for his former fiancée's death. One of Ann's friends, Hannah Cochran, wrote her husband that some of Ann's closest friends were calling Buchanan a "murderer."

In a letter written to Robert Coleman on December 10, Buchanan's devastation and grief appeared obvious: "I feel that happiness has fled from me forever."

In the same missive, Buchanan asked Ann's father for permission to join the procession following her casket to the cemetery. Years later, after Buchanan's own death, the letter was discovered in his personal papers, indicating it was never sent or returned unopened. Regardless of the missive's fate, Buchanan did not attend Ann's funeral or graveside services.

Did Buchanan's tragic romance with Ann Coleman traumatize him to the extent he committed himself to a life of bachelorhood? Buchanan, no doubt, was distraught, destroying all correspondence received from his former fiancée.

While King's story of unrequited love did not end in tragedy, the experience nonetheless left him sad and embarrassed. During his service as Legation Secretary for the American Minister to Russia, 31-year-old King apparently fell in love with Princess Charlotte of Prussia. Charlotte who was 12 years younger than King and destined to become Empress Alexandra Feodorovna was already engaged to Grand Duke Nicholas Alexander, heir to the throne of the Russian Empire.

In the weeks prior to their July 1917 royal wedding at the Grand Church of the Winter Palace, King attended a reception honoring the couple. When King greeted the czarina, he not only kissed her hand but also grasped it for a conspicuous length of time. Some observers judged his behavior inappropriate and perhaps scandalous.

"You will land in Siberia if you aren't careful!" a fellow member of the American diplomatic delegation informed King.

King immediately realized his impulsive show of affection could potentially damage cordial relations between America and Russia. The following morning, he rushed to the Czar's palace to offer an apology to the future wife of Emperor Nicholas I. To his surprise, King was presented with a note from Princess Charlotte stating she had taken no offense to his behavior and welcoming him to visit the palace in the future.

While relieved his passionate indiscretion did not precipitate a diplomatic crisis, King was devastated and seemingly scarred for life. He soon asked Foreign Minister Pinkney for permission to return to the U.S. While King kept a detailed private journal documenting his prior experiences in Europe, he failed to make entries while in Russia or later destroyed those pages.

Bessie Hogan Williams, King's grandniece, later shared what she learned from older family members: "King's feelings for the Czar's [future] daughter [-in-law] grew to be stronger than friendship, and that he was unable to marry her, he vowed to marry no one."

While the two were never involved in a romantic relationship, King remained infatuated with the memory of Princess Charlotte for years to come. More than once, he reminisced about what might have been.

Alabama Governor Israel Pickens was among those who recalled King's lament: "Mine is a wayward heart, that loves but once and loves forever."

Buchanan was scarred and likely felt a measure of guilt over the failed relationship with Ann Coleman ending in death, perhaps by her own hand. While King's burden was much different, it nonetheless haunted him for years.

A vow of bachelorhood appears to be an extreme reaction to lost or unrequited love. Did King and Buchanan use those experiences as convenient excuses for never marrying? Or did they suffer lifelong emotional pain? Most often, King and Buchanan viewed the world through an all or nothing prism. If lone negative romantic experiences can sour individuals on the institute of marriage, King and Buchanan would have been prime candidates.

As is common in close relationships, King and Buchanan tended to complement each other's weaknesses. Chivalrous and brave, King's demeanor was generally serious and reserved. Buchanan was quite the opposite, outgoing and charismatic. While many observers considered his mannerisms effeminate and sometimes odd, Buchanan not only possessed a well-developed sense of humor but also enjoyed socializing and savoring fine wines.

King and Buchanan also served as mentors to some of their full or half-orphaned nieces and nephews. By middle-age, both established particularly close bonds with one of their nieces. At his home in Pennsylvania, Buchanan proudly displayed portraits of his favorite niece, Harriet Rebecca Lane, as well as King's closest niece, Catherine

Margaret Ellis.

King and Buchanan were raised by nurturing mothers with whom they fostered enduring bonds. In contrast, William King Sr. and James Buchanan Sr. were more distant and reserved. Both of their fathers also died at relatively young ages.

As young adults, King and Buchanan sought guidance from older male mentors. Respective role models helped the pair develop skills necessary to achieve financial, occupational, and political success.

In like fashion, King and Buchanan read for the law under the guidance of experienced attorneys rather than attend law school. In addition to common Scots-Irish ancestry, they shared a passion for reading, particularly poetry.

King and Buchanan were never shy about expressing their love of country and openly displaying patriotism. King was a leading proponent of armed conflict with England prior to the onset of the War of 1812. During the ensuing conflict, Buchanan joined the Pennsylvania State Militia, commanded by Judge Harry Shippen. The aptly named Shippen Guards marched to Baltimore but narrowly missed confrontation with the enemy who had already passed though the city in route to ransacking and burning Washington, D.C. King was also a militia member who saw no combat action but attained the rank of Colonel, which became his life-long civilian moniker.

Both were active Free Masons. (King's involvement membership in the fraternal brotherhood was discussed in Chapter 1). In December 1816, Buchanan joined Lancaster's Masonic Lodge Number 43. After a dozen years passed, he was 1st District Deputy Grandmaster for Southern Pennsylvania. From a religious perspective, both men attended Episcopal churches.

In addition to serving abroad as Foreign Ministers, King and Buchanan were politically ambitious lawmakers who aspired to national office. On more than one occasion, the pair dreamed of appearing together on national ballots. While the so-called "bachelor ticket," Buchanan for President and King for Vice-President, never came to fruition, both eventually attained their respective goals with different running mates. King won the Vice-Presidency in 1852, and Buchanan was elected President in 1856.

Each man encountered squabbles within his respective state's political party and adopted less than popular positions among regional peers. As a Moderate Democrat, King sought to promote unity between the North and South. He never embraced the pro-secessionist, fire-eating mantra of many fellow slaveholders. In like fashion, dough-faced Buchanan was more politically and socially comfortable with slave-owning Southerners than anti-slavery Northerners.

King and Buchanan were ardent supporters of President Andrew Jackson. Both remained Jacksonian Democrats well after Old Hickory completed his two terms as President.

As fellow U.S. Senators, the pair voted in unison *88 percent* of the time. Buchanan's positions on significant issues evolved to the extent that he eventually joined King in rejecting the National Bank and supporting establishment of an independent subtreasury system and opposing high protective tariffs which negatively impacted less affluent Americans. Both supported westward migration by white settlers. Despite earlier reservations, Buchanan would ultimately become a much greater devotee of Manifest Destiny than King. Even though they hailed from different regions of the country, King and Buchanan equally detested Abolitionists.

King's and Buchanan's commonalities and shared experiences significantly outnumbered their personal and political differences. Removing rumored sexual and romantic attraction from the equation, the groundwork was laid for an enduring *platonic friendship*.

Historians and biographers who contend King and Buchanan were gay lovers place considerable emphasis on a *single paragraph* of *one letter* written by Buchanan. In May 1844, shortly after King was appointed Foreign Minister to France, Buchanan penned a missive to their mutual friend Cornelia Roosevelt. Roosevelt and her husband had recently hosted King in their New York City home prior to his trans-Atlantic voyage.

In this letter, Buchanan bemoaned King's distant assignment: "I am now *solitary and alone*, having no companion in the house with me. I have gone a *wooing* to several gentlemen but have not succeeded with any of them. I feel that it is not good for a man to be alone, and I should not be astonished to find myself married to some old maid who can nurse me when I am sick, provide good dinners for me when I am well, and not expect from me any very ardent or romantic affection."

Was Buchanan simply expressing loneliness when he wrote this passage? Or did the choice of words reveal covert details about his relationship with King? At first glance, the phraseology suggests King and Buchanan may have been lovers.

A closer examination of Buchanan's words, however, supports different interpretations. In that era, "wooing" was never a word exclusive to heterosexual courtships. Lawmakers were known to *woo* their colleagues when attempting to facilitate political alliances.

The term "solitary and alone" also had shared political roots. In January 1837, Missouri Senator Thomas Hart Benton supported King's successful resolution to expunge the Whig Party's censure resolution against Andrew Jackson as punishment for his refusal to re-charter the National Bank.

Speaking from the floor of the Senate, Benton proclaimed: "*Solitary and alone*, and amidst the jeers and taunts of my opponents, I put this motion forward."

A Whig cartoonist lampooned Benson, depicting him as a tumble bug towing the "Expunging Resolution," which was inscribed with the names of a supporting list of "Black Knights." The names on the resolution included King and Buchanan who were among Senator Benson's boarding house roommates.

King and Buchanan not only shared profound respect for Benson but also were his close friends. Interestingly, the coupling of *solitary* and *alone* appeared more than once in correspondence King and Buchanan sent to other lawmakers.

In his letter to Cornelia Roosevelt, Buchanan bleakly described the prospects of future marriage. Nonetheless, Buchanan, and King to a much lesser degree, were openly flirtatious with certain women. On more than one occasion Buchanan spoke of romantic interests in women, even when cohabitating with King.

In March 1842, Buchanan contemplated marriage to a much younger woman who was living in Tennessee. He ultimately ended the relationship by sending her a poetic letter.

"A match of age with youth can only bring the farce of winter dancing with spring. Blooming nineteen can never well agree with the dull age of half century," he wrote when ending the relationship.

Two years later, 55-year-old Buchanan wrote Matilda Childress Catron, wife of U.S. Supreme Court Justice John Catron, about ending his bachelorhood: "I intend to make one more attempt to change my wretched condition, and should I fail under these auspices, I shall then surrender in despair."

In 1845, Secretary of State Buchanan yet again engaged in playful flirtation. The object of his affections was JoAnna Lucinda Rucker, niece of President Polk. Despite their age difference, the two became quite close.

"You are a girl after my own heart, and I can never forget you," Buchanan wrote Rucker before ultimately ending is courtship.

For many years, Buchanan maintained a close relationship with widowed former First Lady Dolley Madison. Many of Madison's friends and close acquaintances believed she was very much interested in marrying Buchanan, who was 23 years younger. Buchanan, however, was far more interested in pursuing a romantic relationship with Madison's niece, 25-year-old Anna Coles Payne. While the couple never married, Buchanan referred to the younger woman as "lovely Miss Annie."

Approaching age 60, Buchanan continued flirtations with much younger women. One of his targets was the 27-year-old daughter of the Librarian of Congress.

In early 1850, Buchanan went as far as expressing romantic interest in one of King's nieces. After Margaret William King, age 19, visited her uncle in Washington, D.C., Buchanan, ended a missive by requesting King "give my love to Margaret."

"Margaret sends her love," King wrote back.

While *give my love* does not necessarily imply romance, King upped the ante by urging Buchanan to travel to Alabama to "seek and win her," hardly advice expected from one's alleged male lover. Like so many times before, Buchanan's amorous interest in Margaret waned.

It is impossible to know if any of Buchanan's romantic interests in women were genuine or involved sexual intimacy. It is equally risky to definitively label him gay, bisexual, heterosexual, or asexual. In the end, Buchanan's perpetual indecisiveness may have been the most important factor preventing him from committing to long-term romantic relationships with either sex.

While King was living in France and serving as American Foreign Minister, he began to question Buchanan's devotion to their friendship. King was clearly angry and hurt by Buchanan's refusal to maintain regular correspondence while he was living abroad. King eventually wrote a letter sharing his displeasure.

"I had sworn in my wrath that I would never again employ my almost disabled hand in writing you, until you condescended to give me an answer," King tartly penned in one letter, referencing his painful bouts of rheumatism.

After several months passed without a reply from Buchanan, King briefly attempted to rationalize his discontent, suggesting letters written by Buchanan might have been lost in transit while crossing the Atlantic Ocean: "My pride, to say nothing of friendship, brings me to this conclusion."

In the same missive, King expressed dismay over receiving "not a single line since I have been in France." In Buchanan's defense, he was then serving as President Polk's Secretary of State and heavily involved in annexation of Texas and the Canadian border controversy. Nonetheless, Buchanan was a poor correspondent and seemingly ignored his long-time friend's sense of neglect.

When Buchanan sent King a case of Madeira wine by steamship, the gesture partially assuaged his friend's hurt and anger. Spirits temporarily boosted, King wrote a letter expressing hope Buchanan would visit Paris and "enjoy the gayeties of this city of pleasure." Later in the missive, however, King once again reprimanded his friend. He informed Buchanan that "in spite of all your neglect, I still cling with fondness to our ancient friendship."

As Secretary of State and King's immediate boss, Buchanan maintained regular official diplomatic correspondence. Buchanan, however, did not write a single personal letter to King for the first *nine months* his friend resided in France.

After receiving a long-awaited personal letter from Buchanan, King replied with a mix of anxiety and disappointment: "I had come to the conclusion that our friendly intercourse was destined to die a natural death."

When Buchanan neglected to pen a return missive, King grew peevish: "Now as my last four [letters] have commanded no attention, it seems to be time that I should take the hint and annoy you no more."

King's disappointment in Buchanan was not entirely limited to his time in France. In years past, King had been exasperated by his friend's lax communication. In June 1837, while King was at home in Alabama recovering from a near fatal carriage accident, he wrote a stinging letter to Buchanan, who was reportedly preoccupied by yet another flirtatious dalliance with a younger woman.

"Are you so engrossed by aspirations of ambition, or the hopes and anxieties of love, that friendship can find no abiding place in your heart? Or have you been standing on your dignity and waiting to receive the first card?" King frustratingly wrote. (Interestingly, King differentiated love from friendship in this letter).

While King and Buchanan never completely severed ties, the

intimacy of their friendship clearly diminished with the passage of time. The reason for this distancing appears largely one-sided. Buchanan appeared more self-centered and may have adopted the mantra, "out of sight, out of mind." It is also possible he determined King was far too needy.

While both men harbored higher political aspirations, King invariably promoted his friend's quest for the Presidency much more than Buchanan gave in return. No doubt, King was far more invested in maintaining their long-standing friendship when the two were living apart.

While some historians and biographers have flatly opined King and Buchanan were gay lovers, confirmatory evidence is lacking. Contemporary personal and political enemies were responsible for propagating many suggestive and salacious rumors about the bachelor statesmen and could hardly be regarded as objective observers.

If King and Buchanan shared a relationship that involved physical intimacy, any direct proof was clearly hidden. At that point in American history, same-gender relationships were strictly taboo. Prior to the American Revolution, sodomy was a crime punishable by death. At the height of King's and Buchanan's friendship and lengthy cohabitation in the early- to mid-19th Century, individuals convicted of engaging in same sex acts were often sentenced to life imprisonment. Aside from the issue of criminality, definitive proof of a same-gender relationship between King and Buchanan would have led to social ostracization and political suicide. Would either ambitious politician have been willing to make a potentially career-ending sacrifice to gratify their libidos?

Without proof, rumor and innuendo intended to wound or shame others remain nothing more than malicious allegations.

7

Return to Capitol Hill

In the fall of 1846, after a two-year stay in France, King arrived back in the United States. After stopping briefly in Washington, D.C. for an exit interview with President Polk, King headed to Alabama intent upon reviving his political career.

In May 1847, King was unanimously elected Chairman of the Alabama State Democratic Convention. When convention delegates suggested he run for Governor, King immediately declined. He was squarely focused on returning to the U.S. Senate.

After King resigned his Senate seat in 1844, Dixon Hall Lewis was elected to replace him. A rotund 330 pounds, baby-faced Lewis was easily recognizable by his girth and trademark stove pipe hat. Born in Dinwiddie County, Virginia in 1802, Lewis graduated from South Carolina College in 1820. (The college would later be renamed the University of South Carolina). Later that year, like King, he relocated to Alabama.

After reading for the law under tutelage of an attorney who practiced in Cahaba, Lewis was admitted to the bar. He subsequently opened his own law practice in Montgomery, married, and fathered seven children.

In 1826, Lewis entered the arena of politics when he was elected to the Alabama State House of Representatives. At the time, 24-year-old

Lewis was the youngest member of the legislative body. In addition to serving three consecutive terms in the State Legislature, he was a member of the University of Alabama Board of Trustees from 1828-1831, the same time the university was under active construction.

Likeable, witty, charismatic, and a polished orator, Lewis was popular with fellow lawmakers. Despite his intelligence and charm, Lewis was unable to control his obesity. Consequently, he was forced to travel aboard a heavily reinforced carriage, and when the State Legislature was in session, occupied an oversized, custom-made chair.

A Conservative Democrat and States' Righter, Lewis opposed federal government mandates. While never an ardent proponent of secession, he nonetheless believed America was composed of a *voluntary union* of states and secession a Constitutional right.

In 1828, Lewis was elected to the U.S. House of Representatives. Two years later, he was re-elected, defeating Alabama Governor John Murphy. After being voted out of office in 1832, Lewis was again elected in 1834 and proceeded to serve five consecutive terms in the House.

When King left the U.S. Senate in 1844 to serve as Foreign Minister to France, Lewis immediately resigned from the House and was elected to fill the Senate vacancy. Respected and well-liked by his colleagues, Lewis served as Chairman of the Committees of Finance and Entrenchment. (The Entrenchment or Entrenched clause of the U.S. Constitution empowers Congress to determine the ease or difficulty of passing legislative proposals or amendments. Entrenched clauses cannot be overridden absent a supermajority vote, special referendum, or consent from the minority party).

While serving in Congress, Lewis continued to gain weight, surpassing the 400-pound mark. When unable to travel in his own heavy-duty carriage, Lewis was required to book two seats on standard stage coaches. As had been the case when he served in the Alabama State Legislature, Lewis occupied a jumbo-sized chair on the floor of the U.S. Senate.

On one occasion, humorous were it not so sad, Lewis was traveling from Alabama to Washington, D.C. when the floor of the stage coach collapsed beneath his weight. After the rotund Senator was abruptly deposited atop a Georgia road, the incident became a permanent fixture in the Senate's colorful lore.

As the 1846 mid-term elections neared, King was confident he would reclaim his Senate seat. He boldly informed his niece, Catherine Margaret, that "a very large proportion" of Alabamians were desirous of his returning to office, "and unless their representatives play the people false, my election is certain."

King, however, underestimated Dixon Lewis' resolve, the growing popularity of Alabama's opposition Whig Party, and significant infighting among state Democrats. While King supported the non-sectional policies of President Polk, Lewis and his "Chivalry Faction" were ardent States' Righters who regarded South Carolina's legendary and controversial John C. Calhoun as their role model. When the Alabama State Legislature voted to return Lewis to office, King suffered his *first and only defeat* in an election for federal office.

Thought temporarily side-lined from direct participation in national policy-making, King closely monitored the ongoing Mexican-American War. Unlike many expansionist-minded Southern Democrats, King did not consider annihilation of the Mexican Army as one of America's prouder moments.

"Close this Mexican War at the earliest practible [sic] moment; and upon any terms which do not conflict with the honor of the country. Abandon if it is not entertained, the idea of acquiring extensive territory," King wrote his friend, Secretary of State Buchanan.

King's advice fell on deaf ears. By now, Buchanan had come to fully embrace Manifest Destiny. In response to King's letter, Buchanan curtly noted the Mexican government "can conclude a treaty at any moment."

King strongly believed the fighting should end with America

demonstrating ability to "show our magnanimity, and thus free ourselves from the charge of being a grasping nation, readying to seize upon the Territory of our weaker neighbors regardless of right or justice." The justness of Manifest Destiny was one of the rare differences of opinion between King and Buchanan.

At the conclusion of the Mexican-American War, Nicholas Trist, Chief Clerk of the U.S. State Department, was tasked with negotiating terms of surrender. On February 14, 1848, Trist presented Secretary of State Buchanan with the Treaty of Guadalupe Hidalgo. The treaty, namesake of the town where it was drafted, had been signed by American and Mexican negotiators 12 days earlier.

On March 18 that year, the U.S. Senate, by a margin of 38-14, passed the treaty. A day later, Mexican lawmakers approved the agreement, 51-34.

The treaty required Mexico to cede *55 percent* of its cumulative territory. Those lands would eventually become all or part of present-day New Mexico, Arizona, Utah, Nevada, Colorado, Wyoming, and California. Mexico also agreed to relinquish any claims to Texas. In addition, the Rio Grande River was established as Texas' permanent southern border. In return, the U.S. not only paid Mexico $15,000,000 for the ceded territory but also took over responsibility for reimbursing American citizens for debts owed to them by the Mexican government. The treaty further permitted all Mexicans who remained in ceded territories for at least one year be granted full American citizenship and guaranteed civil rights.

In 1853, the Gadsden Purchase added to America's territorial expansion. The 29,640 square miles acquired from Mexico at a cost of $10,000,000 became portions of modern-day New Mexico and Arizona.

As a Southern slaveholder, King vehemently opposed the Wilmot Proviso. Introduced by Pennsylvania Congressman David Wilmot in 1846, the bill would have prohibited spread of slavery into territories acquired by the U.S. after the Mexican-American War. Many Northern Democrats, including Buchanan, joined ranks with their Southern colleagues in voting against the legislative proposal. Consequently, Northern Whigs were the only majority supporters of the measure. The Wilmot Proviso was twice passed by the House of Representatives, but enough Senate Democrats voted against the legislation to keep it from being enacted into law.

During his tenure as Secretary of State, Buchanan steadfastly supported Manifest Destiny and westward expansion of slavery. He also peacefully negotiated a permanent border between the northern Oregon Territory and Canada. Buchanan's notable diplomatic successes on two critical fronts improved his Presidential prospects.

On June 16, 1848, less than two years after incumbent Dixon Hall Lewis thwarted King's bid to regain his seat in Congress, Alabama Senator Arthur Pendleton Bagby resigned to accept appointment as Foreign Minister to Russia. Born in Virginia in 1794, Bagby migrated to Alabama to practice law and become a cotton planter. The slaveholding attorney served in the State House of Representatives before he was elected as Alabama's 10th Governor. On November 21, 1841, Governor Bagby appointed himself to fill the vacancy created by the resignation of Senator Clement Comer Clay.

After Bagby resigned his Senate seat, Alabama Governor Reuben Chapman appointed King to fill the vacancy. At first, King feared Senator Lewis would attempt to block his appointment out of "personal hostility," but the rotund lawmaker, secure in his own seat, voiced no opposition.

Washington D.C. and the entire country had changed considerably from the time King began his Congressional career. When first elected to the U.S. Senate in 1820, the Union consisted of only 22 states. By 1848, the number had grown to 30, including newly admitted Wisconsin.

The dominant political issues of the day were also different.

Controversy over the National Bank and high protective tariffs had been eclipsed by sectional divide over the legality and morality of slavery. The slavery debate would only intensify and ultimately outlive King.

After Congress recessed in 1848, King returned to Alabama to seek election for an outright term. During the campaign, King was subjected to criticisms from the state's Conservative Democrats. One opponent ridiculed King's "childish desire to be elected to the Senate." After making tenuous peace with many of Alabama's most ardent pro-secessionist States' Righters, King was elected by the State Legislature to a full term in the U.S. Senate.

That same year, 46-year-old, 430-pound Senator Dixon Hall Lewis traveled to New York City to seek medical care for mounting physical problems, aggravated by morbid obesity. While in New York, Lewis' health rapidly declined, culminating in his death on October 25, 1848. After an elaborate funeral, Lewis' remains were interred in Brooklyn's Greenwood Cemetery. Alabama lawmakers subsequently elected former two-term Governor Benjamin Fitzpatrick to fill the vacant Senate seat.

Following outright election to the U.S. Senate, King hosted a victory celebration at Montgomery's Exchange Hotel. Recovering from a "severe cold," he remained in Alabama for several days before departing for Washington, D.C. During King's extended stay in Montgomery, he witnessed a raging fire that destroyed the State Capitol Building. (Just two years earlier, Montgomery had been designated as Alabama's permanent capital).

After his health improved, King began the nearly 700-mile trek to the nation's capital. The arduous journey necessitated travel by stagecoach, boat, and train.

Most of King's Democratic colleagues warmly welcomed his return to the 30th Congress in late 1848, corresponding with the lame duck months of President Polk's single term. Fellow lawmakers discovered King's determination, work ethic, and negotiation skills remained unchanged.

Albert James Pickett was one of King's chief admirers. Born in North Carolina, Pickett was an attorney and cotton planter who eventually settled in Alabama's south-central Autauga County. In 1851, Pickett published a two-volume history of his adopted state, earning the title, "Alabama's first historian."

"Colonel King has maintained a spotless reputation; his frank and confiding disposition, his uniform courtesy and kindness, has endured him to numerous friends," Pickett wrote in his tome.

Perhaps still angry and hurt by James Buchanan's unwillingness to maintain regular private correspondence while he was living in France, King sought different accommodations. Instead of rooming with Buchanan, he rented a boarding house room near Capitol Hill. King's newly acquired messmates were largely fellow Southern lawmakers, including Mississippi Senator Jefferson Davis, future President of the Confederate States of America. Mrs. Davis, who accompanied her husband to the capital city, was impressed by King, describing him as "a man as elegant as he was sound and sincere."

During the brief Congressional session, King, having overcome prior misgivings about James K. Polk's leadership abilities, remained loyal to the outgoing President. King was soon appointed to the Joint Congressional Committee responsible for accepting Polk's Final Annual Address to lawmakers.

While no longer living under the same roof, King and Buchanan nonetheless maintained a cordial relationship. On December 14, the pair arrived together at a formal White House dinner honoring Polk's Cabinet members and Congressional Democratic leaders.

During his second stint in Congress, King served as Chairman of the prestigious Senate Committees on Foreign Relations and Pensions. For the remainder of his Senate career, King would be recognized as a leader and conciliator.

In 1848, the same year King returned to the Senate, voters elected a new President. The Democratic nomination was a wide-open affair after Polk committed to serving only a single term.

Buchanan and King were considered legitimate candidates for the Presidency and Vice-Presidency, respectively. Several pro-Democratic newspapers published articles endorsing a "bachelor ticket."

Buchanan, however, initially honored an earlier commitment. In 1845, hoping to prevent infighting within his Administration, President Polk informed each Cabinet member that if they planned to run for President or Vice-President in 1848, he would accept their immediate resignations. Buchanan soon announced he would make no "personal exertions" for the Democratic Presidential nomination.

King, on the other hand, faced no impediments in his quest for higher office. In early 1848, delegates attending the Alabama Democratic Party Convention in Montgomery nominated him as a Vice-Presidential candidate.

In the weeks and months leading up to the Democratic National Convention, King refused to believe Buchanan would honor his previous pledge not to seek the Presidential nomination. King tried to muster support for Buchanan, publicly lauding Polk's Secretary of State as the "Atlas of the Administration." He further informed Buchanan that his own niece, Catherine Margaret, was eager to "hear you deliver your inaugural from the front of the Capitol in 1849."

By the time the Democratic National Convention opened in Baltimore on May 26, a physically and emotionally exhausted President Polk had already endorsed Lewis Cass, Michigan Senator and former U.S. Army General, as his successor. On the 4th ballot, Cass won the requisite 2/3rd majority of delegate votes. Cass outdistanced several candidates, including U.S. Supreme Court Associate Justice Levi Woodbury of New Hampshire and Buchanan, the latter having eventually *allowed* his name to be placed into nomination.

King's quest for the Vice-Presidential nomination was equally frustrating. After the 1st ballot, he was a distant third, trailing former Kentucky U.S. Congressman William O. Butler and John A. Quitman, former fire-eating Governor of Mississippi and U.S. Army General who fought in the Mexican-American War.

King's dream soon ended abruptly. On the 2nd ballot, delegates nominated Butler as the party's Vice-Presidential candidate.

While King and Buchanan still fantasized about a bachelor ticket, time had become a factor. At age 62, King wondered how many chances remained to his achieve goal of becoming Vice-President.

On June 7, the Whig Party National Convention opened in Philadelphia. Future President Abraham Lincoln and his friend Alexander Stephens, a mercurial Georgia Congressman and future Vice-President of the Confederate States of America, were among delegates elected to the convention.

Though his hopes remained high, delegates refused to nominate party stalwart Henry Clay a *fourth* time. While Clay's political resume would never include the Presidency, his legacy remains no less notable. For four decades, the Great Compromiser played a key role in crafting key legislation.

Instead, Whig delegates selected Zachary Taylor, former U.S. Army General and Mexican-American War veteran, as the party's Presidential nominee. Nicknamed "Old Rough and Ready," Taylor had not been a politician long enough to accumulate many enemies. Former New York Congressman Millard Fillmore was nominated as Taylor's running mate. With a well-regarded war hero heading the ticket, Whigs were excited by the prospect of winning the White House. Their hopes were soon transformed into reality.

In the November General Election, Taylor defeated Cass and former President Martin Van Buren, candidate of upstart Free Soil Party, to become the 12th President of the United States. Taylor won a 47.3 percent plurality in the popular vote, carried 15 states, and tallied 163 electoral votes. Finishing second, Cass won 42.5 percent of the vote, carried 15 states, and amassed 127 electoral votes. Capturing only 10.1

percent of the popular vote, Van Buren failed to carry any states or win any electoral votes. (The Free Soilers' third-party existence spanned 1848-1864 before most members joined the nascent Republican Party).

Free Soilers focused largely on a single issue, opposing expansion of slavery into developing western territories. Party members, however, never adopted the moral stance of Abolitionists. Instead, they feared migrating Blacks, free or slave, would deprive white settlers of employment opportunities. Salmon P. Chase, Ohio Governor and United States Senator as well as future unsuccessful Presidential candidate, Secretary of the Treasury in President Abraham Lincoln's Administration, and Chief Justice of the U.S. Supreme Court, was a prominent Free Soiler who later joined the Republican Party).

In June 1850, numerous radical, pro-slavery Southern Democrats congregated for a Unity Convention in Nashville. The main topic of discussion was secession from the Union. Ever the conciliator and Moderate Democrat, King had unsuccessfully attempted to block the convention. When Southern fire-eaters met in Tennessee's capital city, delegates were not yet willing to pull the trigger of secession and arrived at little consensus about preserving States' Rights and maintaining slavery.

Even though James Buchanan was a dyed-in-the-wool *Conservative Democrat*, his positions on the two most controversial issues of the day were paradoxical. While professing a personal hatred of slavery, he loathed Abolitionists even more. In addition, Buchanan firmly believed slavery was protected by the Constitution. While opining secession was unconstitutional, Buchanan also proclaimed disunion could not be prevented by the federal government. His logic was most confusing. (A decade later, Buchanan's indecisiveness and contradictions would directly contribute to disunion of the country).

THE 25-DAY VICE-PRESIDENT

On July 4, 1850, just 16 months after he was inaugurated President, 65-year-old Zachary Taylor attended a holiday celebration at the Washington Monument. During the patriotic gala, he consumed copious amounts of cherries and iced milk.

The following day, Taylor began experiencing symptoms consistent with gastroenteritis. Within hours, his condition markedly worsened. Dr. Alexander S. Wotherspoon, the President's personal physician, diagnosed "cholera morbus," an antiquated term for gastrointestinal infection.

Despite treatments implemented by Wotherspoon and consulting physicians, Taylor's condition rapidly deteriorated. At 10:50 p.m., on July 9, just four days after taking ill, the President died.

(Not surprisingly, many conspiracy theorists refuse to believe the President died of natural causes, alleging Taylor was murdered by arsenic poisoning. Totally unrelated groups, including pro-slavery Southerners and discontented Catholics, have been accused of assassinating Taylor.

On June 17, 1991, nearly 141 years after President Taylor's death, his closest living relative granted permission for the former President's body to be exhumed from its burial site, a mausoleum in Louisville, Kentucky. After Taylor's corpse was delivered to the office of the Kentucky Medical Examiner, fingernail, hair, and other tissue samples were collected from his decomposed remains before reinterment of the body. The specimens were then subjected to neutron activation analysis at Tennessee's Oak Ridge National Laboratory. Experts participating in the investigation subsequently concluded there was *no evidence of arsenic poisoning*, and opined Taylor's cause of death was indeed a gastrointestinal infection. Taylor likely contracted the fatal illness after consuming food and drink contaminated with bacteria thriving in Washington, D.C.'s open sewers.

Furthermore, the President's attending physicians likely hastened his demise by administering large doses of ipecac, calomel, quinine, and opium as well as prescribing other common treatment modalities of that era, including bleeding and blistering. Conspiracy theories, however, seldom fade way and almost never expire. In 2010, Michael Parenti, a political scientist, revived the specter of arsenic poisoning after consulting with a group of forensic pathologists. Parenti ambiguously concluded "there is no definitive proof that Taylor was assassinated, nor would it appear that there is no definitive proof that he was not").

On July 11, 1850, two days after Taylor's death and Millard Fillmore's ascension to the Presidency, King's Senate colleagues elected him President Pro Tempore by a rare *unanimous* vote. With the Vice-Presidency now vacant, King was a heartbeat away from the Presidency for the second time in his career.

(On July 18, 1947, President Harry S. Truman signed into law the Presidential Succession Act. A new order of succession to the Presidency, which remains in effect today, was established in sequential fashion: Vice-President, Speaker of the House, and President Pro Tempore of the Senate. If none of the three are capable or willing to serve as President, the line of succession shifts to Cabinet officers in the chronological order of their department's establishment: Secretary of State, Secretary of the Treasury, Attorney General, Secretary of Interior, Secretary of Agriculture, Secretary of Commerce, Secretary of Labor, Secretary of Health and Human Services, Secretary of Housing and Urban Development, Secretary of Transportation, Secretary of Energy, Secretary of Veteran Affairs, and Secretary of Homeland Security).

After he was elected President Pro Tempore for the second time, King vowed to enforce Senate rules "mildly but firmly" and welcomed his "brother Senators, in a spirit of kindness, to correct my errors." King would serve as President Pro Tempore for the remainder of his Senatorial career, to include the 31st and 32nd Congresses.

As settlers progressively migrated to Western territories destined to become states, conflicts between Northerners and Southerners concerning slavery intensified. As a Moderate Southern Democrat, King occupied the lonely existence of conciliator, thanklessly endeavoring to prevent Democratic Party infighting.

As President Pro Tempore, King helped draft and successfully pass the Compromise of 1850. The new law admitted California to the Union as a free state, prohibited anti-slavery laws from being enacted in the Utah and New Mexico Territories (a portion of the lands ceded by Mexico to the United States following the Mexican-American War), banned slave trade but not slavery itself in the District of Columbia, and called for strict enforcement of the Fugitive Slave Act.

The Fugitive Slave Act, passed by Congress in September 1850, required Federal Marshals to return runaway slaves to their masters even if escapees fled to free states. Fugitive slaves were not afforded jury trials and individuals accused of aiding and abetting escapees were subjected to harsh penalties. The Fugitive Slave Act would not be repealed until June 28, 1864, less than a year before the Civil War ended.

The Compromise of 1850 proved to be one of the final Congressional acts orchestrated by Senator Henry Clay. The Great Communicator died of tuberculosis two years later.

Both pro- and anti-slavers benefitted from different aspects of the Compromise of 1850. The addition of California as a free state not only resulted in the election of additional anti-slavery Congressmen and Senators but also balanced the scales after Texas was admitted as slave state. Conversely, Southern plantation owners were pleased by strict enforcement of the Fugitive Slave Act.

Even though he played a key role in passage of the Compromise of 1850, King worried the issue of slavery would eventually lead to dissolution of the Union. In a letter to Buchanan, he questioned the wisdom of having returned to Congress.

"A seat in the Senate, I assure you, far from being desirable to me, bringing with it as does at this particular time especially, great responsibility, great labor, and no little anxiety," he wrote. (Given his passion for public service and love of the Senate, King's sense of foreboding must have been genuine and profound).

Nonetheless, King continued to mediate conflicts between ardent pro- and anti-slavery lawmakers: "I speak as a Senator who has been here many years, and as one always anxious to see other members of this body to behave properly and kindly toward one another."

As Chairman of the Senate Foreign Relations Committee during the 31st Congress, King played a crucial role in shepherding passage of the Clayton-Bulwer Treaty. Signed by the U.S. and Great Britain in 1850, the measure lessened tensions concerning America's proposal to build a canal connecting the Atlantic and Pacific Oceans through the Central American country of Nicaragua.

The treaty specified no such canal would be constructed without cooperation, neither the U.S. nor Great Britain would "fortify or found colonies in the area," and the proposed waterway would remain under neutral control. While the Nicaraguan canal was never constructed, the Clayton-Bulwer Treaty remained in effect until 1901. (Construction of the Panama Canal began in 1903 and the waterway was opened to traffic on August 14, 1914. Under auspices of the Hay-Bunau-Varilla Treaty, the canal and surrounding area remained under American control for much of the 20th Century. In 1977, President Jimmy Carter and Panamanian Dictator Omar Torrijos signed the Panama Canal Treaty. The U.S. Senate debated the controversial measure for more than six months before ratifying the measure. As specified in the treaty, American ownership of the Panama Canal Zone ended on October 1, 1979. On December 31, 1999, full control of the canal and surrounding area was turned over to Panama).

While King supported the Clayton-Bulwer Treaty to foster unity between fellow Democrats, he never embraced unchecked American expansionism. In a letter to Buchanan, King wrote he was "decidedly opposed to any further acquisition of Territory at this time in any quarter."

Buchanan, however, remained devoted to Manifest Destiny. In his reply to King's letter, the former Secretary of State expressed "regret for the first time we differ radically upon a question which I deem of such vast importance as the Nicaraguan Treaty."

Following passage of the Compromise of 1850, the foundation of the Whig Party began cracking. While Whigs struggled to find a suitable candidate for the 1852 Presidential election, Democrats were poised to regain control of the White House.

When King returned to Alabama during a Congressional recess in the fall of 1850, he was once again ostracized by fire-eating Democrats for his moderate positions on States' Rights and secession. Perhaps responding to intrastate pressure, King soon made it known his conciliatory stance was not irrevocable.

"The North should be made to understand that we will bear no more, that another step taken by her to endanger our safety must and will snap the cord which binds us together," he confided to a fellow Alabama Democrat.

Most Southerners, temporarily placated by the Compromise of 1850, were less inclined to push for immediate secession. At the same time, fire-eaters were certain dissolution of the country was an eventuality. King was among those sincerely hoping the Union would somehow persevere.

After returning for the Congressional session convening in early 1851, King invited Buchanan to visit him in Washington, D.C. Two years earlier, Buchanan had purchased a stately manor in Lancaster, Pennsylvania which he christened Wheatland. There, Buchanan maintained a self-imposed facade of *retirement* after serving as Secretary of State.

Accompanied by his niece, Harriet Lane, Buchanan traveled to the nation's capital. King had recently rented rooms at a boarding house on New Jersey Avenue for himself and his nieces, Catherine Margaret Ellis and Margaret William King, both having accompanied him to the capital city. It is not known if Buchanan and Lane occupied King's accommodations during their month-long stay.

Buchanan had ulterior motives for accepting King's generous invitation. The visit enabled him to consult, face-to-face, with potential supporters who informed Buchanan his prospects of winning the Democratic Party Presidential nomination in 1852 were favorable.

After Buchanan returned to Wheatland, he reverted to being an inattentive correspondent. Hurt and angry, King responded in a manner that stung Buchanan where it hurt most.

"Perhaps you suppose I have so little influence that my Friendship is of minor importance. Do not be deceived. I am the only man who can beat you in Alabama; and unless you pay more attention to me, I will have the ticket," King wrote, referencing the coming year's Presidential election.

In the same letter, King reported an Alabama newspaper editor had proposed an 1852 ticket consisting of King for President and former Pennsylvania Senator George Mifflin Dallas as his running mate. While King apparently had no real interest in being elected President, the mere mention of Buchanan's Pennsylvania rival on the Democratic Presidential ticket was certain to rankle him.

King's admonition apparently caught Buchanan's attention. He soon proposed a regular exchange of letters detailing the mindset of Democratic powerbrokers leading up to the 1852 Presidential election.

Suffering from painful bouts of rheumatism, King began dictating some letters to his niece, Catherine Margaret. She then wrote the missives in longhand before mailing them to Buchanan and others.

In January 1852, at King's urging, Buchanan once again visited Washington, D.C. With the Democratic National Convention set to convene in less than six months, Buchanan appeared more eager to spend time with his close friend and perspective Vice-Presidential running mate. King and Buchanan maintained high hopes for the dream bachelor ticket.

Unbeknownst to either man, the 1852 General Election year would be filled with triumph, disappointment, and ominous foreboding.

8

Vice-President King

From the time John Adams was elected as America's first Vice-President until well into the 20th Century, the office was more honorific than substantiative. Presidents delegated few responsibilities to their Vice-Presidents, aside from representing the Executive branch as designated mourners at high profile funerals. Absent assigned office space in or near the White House, Vice-Presidents were literally and figuratively distanced from the President.

Even today, as the chief presiding officer of the Senate, the Vice-President's role is mostly symbolic. A Vice-President's only direct involvement in the legislative process is limited to casting infrequent tie-breaking votes.

What motivated King to seek election to a largely insignificant role in government? He not only regarded the Senate as America's greatest legislative assembly but also considered it an honor to serve as the sole representative straddling the Legislative and Executive branches of federal government. While he appeared content to seek no further political advancement, as President Pro Tempore of the Senate, King was aware he had twice been a heartbeat away from the Presidency following the deaths of William Henry Harrison and Zachary Taylor. In an era when life-expectancy was much shorter than today, King may have harbored secret ambitions to occupy the White House via the backdoor.

THE 25-DAY VICE-PRESIDENT

By election year 1852, the bonds of friendship between King and Buchanan were still strained, a byproduct of the former's neediness and the latter's neglect. Nonetheless, King believed Buchanan was qualified to serve as President of the United States. And he still fantasized about serving as Buchanan's Vice-President. King and Buchanan were both reaching ages when time was more enemy than friend, and their window for a bachelor ticket was rapidly narrowing.

By now, the prospect of King completing even a single term as Vice-President was clearly in jeopardy. At some point, likely while serving as Foreign Minister to France, he contracted tuberculosis. During the time King resided in Paris, the European city was a hotbed for tubercular infections.

In the 1800s, tuberculosis, also referred to as "white death" and "white plague," was a gradually progressing death sentence for many who contracted the contagion. Tuberculosis was as much of a threat to viability as the twin scourges of polio and AIDS would become in the 20th Century. During the early 1800s, tuberculosis was responsible for *25 percent* of all deaths in Europe.

Transmitted by *Mycobacterium tuberculosis*, a germ invisible to the naked eye, tuberculosis was incurable in the pre-antibiotic era. The airborne contagion was passed to unsuspecting victims from individuals infected with active tuberculosis. A single sneeze or wet cough was capable of spewing 40,000 infectious droplets, each 0.5-5 micrometers in diameter.

Most people who inhaled the pathogen displayed no symptoms; a condition known as latent tuberculosis. In such cases, an individual's immune system was strong enough to wall off the contagion in calcified granulomas, usually in the lung or proximate lymph nodes. Those plagued with less robust immune functioning developed the active disease which started in the lungs and often spread elsewhere, including the spine, kidney, and brain. Patients with active tuberculosis experienced chronic bouts of coughing, expectoration of blood-tinged sputum, fevers, night sweats, and profound weight loss.

By early 1852, King was clearly a sick man. He was pallid, coughed frequently, and had lost considerable weight. One of his treating physicians likened his emaciated physique to a skeleton.

Buchanan appeared oblivious to his close friend's declining health, perhaps blinded by personal ambition. Fixated on the forthcoming Democratic National Convention, Buchanan was certain the time had come for him to be elected President of the United States.

Prior to the convention, newspapers in Pennsylvania, Alabama, North Carolina, and Mississippi had already endorsed Buchanan for President and King for Vice-President. The editor of *The Alabama Gazette* proclaimed, "such a ticket would carry every solitary Southern State."

The Pittsburgh Daily Post published an undeniable endorsement: "Democratic Ticket. For President of the United States: James Buchanan of Pennsylvania; Subject to Decision of the Democratic General Convention. For Vice-President: William R. King of Alabama: Subject to the Same Decision."

As the sectional debate over slavery intensified, Democratic politicos were certain regional balance on the ticket was necessary to triumph on Election Day. The bachelor ticket—Buchanan from the North and King from the South—was a solid pairing.

When the Democratic National Convention opened on June 1, 1852, at the Maryland Institute for the Promotion of the Mechanic's Art Hall in Baltimore, Buchanan, Michigan Senator Lewis Cass, and Illinois Senator Stephen Douglas were considered front runners for the Presidential nomination.

After the 1st ballot, Cass accumulated 116 delegate votes compared to 93 for Buchanan. The remaining votes were spread out between Douglas and William L. Marcy, former Governor of New York and Secretary of War during James K. Polk's Administration. From the 10th through the 20th ballots, Buchanan assumed the lead but failed to win the requisite 2/3rd majority.

After the 30th deadlocked ballot was concluded, Buchanan had fallen to third place, trailing both Cass and Douglas. On the 35th ballot, a dark horse candidate, New Hampshire's Franklin Pierce, emerged. A former U.S. Congressman and Senator as well as U.S. Army General, Pierce's political resume was impressive. And even though he was a Northerner, Pierce opposed the Abolitionist movement while supporting the Kansas-Nebraska and Fugitive Slave Acts. Consequently, Southern Democrats found little fault with his candidacy. On the 49th ballot, Pierce finally won enough votes to secure the nomination.

Delegates then followed the established trend of choosing a running mate to maintain sectional balance on the ticket. King, a pro-slavery States' Righter but not a fire-eating secessionist, fit the bill perfectly.

With little suspense, on the first ballot, King's dreams finally came true. He easily defeated Louisiana Senator Solomon Downs to win the Vice-Presidential nomination.

Edmund Burke, Pierce's campaign manager and fellow New Hampshire resident, shared his post-convention stamp of approval with the Democratic Presidential nominee: "I think we did the right thing in putting King on the ticket. You know he is Buchanan's bosom friend, and a great and powerful interest is conciliated."

Even though Buchanan was disappointed about once again failing to secure the Democratic Presidential nomination, party strategists expected him to actively participate in narrowing the breech between Northern and Southern Democrats during the General Election campaign. Buchanan's unpredictable nature, however, was worrisome. Would his long-time friendship with King trump bitter personal disappointment?

Early on, Buchanan appeared to be a team player. He confided to a friend that King "would make an excellent President" if Pierce died or became incapacitated while in office.

"Colonel King is everything he ought to be & I shall give the ticket a cordial support," Buchanan wrote a fellow Democrat.

Buchanan also composed a letter to the editor of *The Washington*

Daily Union: "Of Colonel King, I can say emphatically, that he is one of the purest, the most sound judging Statesmen, I have ever known."

As would have been expected, King proclaimed Pierce was the ideal Presidential nominee. But privately, he was stunned and saddened by Buchanan's convention defeat.

"I would have greatly preferred our Friend Buchanan, but he was set aside," King wrote to a friend.

King directly commiserated with Buchanan via letter: "No Friend of yours could feel more mortification at your failure to obtain the nomination of the Baltimore Convention than I did."

Margaret Catherine Ellis penned a separate missive to Buchanan expressing her uncle's displeasure with delegates who voted for Pierce. She affirmed that King "mourned your defeat."

The Whig Party National Convention, June 16-21, 1852, was also held in Baltimore. By this point in history the party was on its dying legs, fragmented beyond repair over the issue of slavery.

Incumbent President Millard Fillmore and General Winfield Scott, hero of the Mexican-American War, were front runners for the nomination. Fillmore, who ascended to the Presidency after Zachary Taylor's sudden death in 1850, was laden with negative political baggage. His support of the Compromise of 1850 and the Fugitive Slave Act alienated him from most Northern Whigs.

Scott, Commanding General of the United States Army from 1841-1861, emerged as a rising political star following the war with Mexico. Scott, however, vehemently opposed slavery, alienating most Southern Whigs.

After 53 contentious ballots, Scott ultimately won the party's Presidential nomination. North Carolina's William A. Graham, former U.S. Senator, Governor, and President Fillmore's Secretary of the Navy, was nominated as Scott's running mate after only two ballots.

The ineffectual Free Soil Party, focused on keeping African Americans from settling into western territories, appealed to only a tiny portion of the electorate. With little chance of winning the Presidency, the third party nominated New Hampshire Senator John P. Hale.

During the General Election season, Buchanan regressed to a state of pettiness. He not only ceased written correspondence with King but also refused to campaign on behalf of the Democratic Presidential ticket. Cloistered in his Wheatland estate, Buchanan was essentially a bitter and silent bystander.

By the summer of 1852, King's tuberculosis had worsened to the point he could not actively campaign. Too sick to travel, King was forced to cancel a scheduled rally in his birth state of North Carolina. Following the advice of his personal physician, he began searching for "some quiet watering place in the mountains, where pure air and rest, it is hoped, speedily restores me to health." Any possibility of *cure*, however, was illusory.

Buchanan's response to King's deteriorating health was puzzling. He apparently made no effort to contact his ailing friend. Was Buchanan too grief stricken to reach out? Or was he narcissistically self-absorbed? Perhaps King's nomination for Vice-President was a painful reminder of his own convention defeat. Regardless of the root cause, Buchanan abandoned King when his friend most needed support from family and friends.

After receiving a letter from their mutual friend Rose O'Neal Greenhow, Buchanan shared a modicum of sadness: "I am sorry to hear that Col. King is looking badly. He is a man of a thousand. He has always been my friend, through good & evil report."

Meanwhile, politicos and members of the press focused on a Presidential campaign featuring the "Battle of Generals." Both Winfield Scott and Franklin Pierce had served as officers during the Mexican-American War. As a Brigadier General, however, Pierce was subordinate in rank to Scott and received fewer public accolades.

In an era predating Presidential preference polls, Democratic Party advertisements reflected the tone of established front runners: "WE

POLKED YOU IN '44, AND WE SHALL PIERCE YOU IN '52."

The Grand National Democratic banner was more dignified, featuring photographs captioned "Pierce for President" and "William R. King for Vice-President." The top of the banner read: "IN UNION IS STRENGTH," while the bottom portion was inscribed, "THE UNION NOW AND FOREVER."

While an ailing King remained distant from the campaign, fellow politicians and newspaper editors focused on two divergent themes when referencing him. Supporters touted King's unblemished record as a public servant while opponents revived salacious and speculative rumors underlying King's lifelong bachelorhood.

A pro-Democratic newspaper, *The Brooklyn Eagle*, while firmly supporting King's candidacy, nonetheless injected an unnecessary barb: "Mr. King is a man of fortune and a bachelor; but he is so mature in years, that we suspect he will not be carried off by the ladies, should he be elevated to the dignified position to which his party has named him."

Amid snickers and laughter while speaking at a campaign rally, William Smith, former Democratic Governor of Virginia, simultaneously endorsed and poked fun at King: "I know him well, love him dearly, and am proud to be called one of his friends. To be sure, he has never brought a woman to his bosom, but he is nonetheless kind and attractive in his disposition."

King's political enemies, whether it be opposition party Whigs or Southern fire-eating Democrats, predictably referenced his *presumed* taboo sexual orientation. A pro-Whig newspaper editor opined King's "distinguished" reputation was due to his having "the smallest foot of any man in the United States Senate." Another partisan publication proclaimed the Vice-Presidential nominee was made of "flimsy, tinselly sort of stuff that is intended rather to be admired than handled."

The New York Times quoted the late John Randolph, a Democratic-Republican Senator from Virginia: "Mr. King? Why madam, Mr. King wears the handsomest pair of boots in Washington."

THE 25-DAY VICE-PRESIDENT

◦∽◦

On Election Day, November 2, 1852, *69.5 percent* of eligible voters cast their ballots for President. The Democrats handily defeated their opponents. Franklin Pierce, age 47, and 66-year-old William R. King won 50.8 percent of popular vote, carried 27 states, and amassed 254 electoral votes. The Scott/Graham Whig pairing finished a distant second—43.9 percent of the popular vote, four states, and 42 electoral votes. John P. Hale, the Free Soil candidate, tallied a mere 5.3 percent of the popular vote, carried no states, and won zero electoral votes.

Election year 1852 also marked the end of an era. The Whig Party faded into oblivion over slavery. The Republican Party soon emerged as the only major party to challenge Democrats from that time forward.

Pierce's election as President also coincided with virtual extinction of Moderate Southern Democrats. As civil war loomed on the horizon, secessionists took control of State Democratic Parties south of the Mason-Dixon Line.

◦∽◦

On December 11, 1852, James Buchanan emerged from his pity party long enough to write President-Elect Pierce a letter praising King: "He is among the best, purest, and most consistent public men I have ever known, and is also a sound-judging and discreet counselor. You might rely with implicit confidence upon his information, especially in regard to the Southern States, which I know are at present trembling alive to the importance of your Cabinet selections."

There is no evidence Pierce acknowledged Buchanan's letter. In that era, collaborative relationships between Presidents and Vice-Presidents were essentially non-existent. In the four months separating Election and Inauguration Days, King's declining health prevented him from traveling to meet with Pierce, who was closeted with close advisors in his home state of New Hampshire.

In a letter to Buchanan, King confirmed Pierce's disinterest in receiving advice or feedback from his Vice-President-Elect: "I am not one of those whom he takes into his confidence, for not a single line have I received from him since his nomination."

King was further disappointed when Pierce failed to appoint Buchanan Secretary of State or consider him for another Cabinet office. Absent any communication from the President-Elect, Buchanan disingenuously but forlornly informed a friend that he planned to "gracefully & gradually retire from public view."

In addition to displeasure at being ignored, King privately expressed "little confidence" in Pierce's primary advisers. He also believed the President-Elect was blatantly disregarding much of the party platform by ignoring Southern Democrats, which would only worsen existing sectional divide.

King, however, was dealing with a far bigger issue than politics. Terminally ill, he was unable to appreciate, much less savor, election to an office so long coveted. Unfortunately, medical professionals had little to offer patients suffering from active tuberculosis other than spending time in climates deemed more hospitable to declining pulmonary functioning.

On December 20, 1852, King submitted a letter dictated to and written by his niece, Catherine Margaret, tendering his resignation from the U.S. Senate. In the farewell missive, he thanked legislative colleagues for their "uniform personal kindness and the general support you have never failed to give me in my efforts to preserve order and enforce parliamentary law."

King was dismayed when Senator David Rice Atchison was elected President Pro Tempore. He was rightfully concerned the fire-eating Missouri Democrat would utilize his leadership position to widen the breech between Northern and Southern party members. King feared his efforts as a Moderate Democrat and sectional conciliator would eventually disappear in clouds of battlefield artillery and rifle smoke.

Worse yet, King was forced to focus on his declining health and mortality. Following his physicians' recommendations, King looked toward Cuba as the best location for palliative care. If lucky, the island's temperate climate and salt air might prolong his life and ease suffering.

On January 1, 1853, Catherine Margaret composed a letter dictated by her uncle and mailed to Buchanan: "He requests me to inform you of his proposed departure, and of his sincere desire to see you before he leaves. Uncle desires me to give you his affectionate remembrances."

However, neither man attempted to arrange a face-to-face meeting prior to King leaving the country. In reality, there was hardly time for Buchanan to travel from Pennsylvania to Alabama and bid his friend adieu. It is also possible neither was emotionally equipped to say goodbye for what might be the final time.

On January 22, King and Catherine Margaret boarded an American warship, *The U.S.S. Fulton*, in Alabama's port city of Mobile for the voyage to Cuba. While Franklin Pierce had ignored King since Election Day, he nonetheless graciously arranged for the Vice-President-Elect to travel aboard a Navy steamship. Pierce displayed more compassion than Buchanan, who apparently never replied to King's missive announcing his departure for Cuba.

King and Catherine Margaret spent their first 16 days in Havana. Afterwards, the pair traveled to the coastal community of Matanzas, roughly 50 miles east of the capital city, and settled at La Adriana, one of many sugar cane plantations located in the area.

King's illness precluded his return to Washington, D.C. for the traditional inaugural ceremony. On March 2, 1853, Congress passed a special resolution to accommodate King's unique situation.

On March 24, Judge William Sharkey, America's Consul General to Cuba, administered the oath of office to the 13th Vice-President of the United States at the Municipal Palace in Matanzas. It marked the first and only time in American history that a President or Vice-President has been sworn into office on foreign soil.

Shortly after her uncle's remote inauguration, Catherine Margaret self-composed a letter to Buchanan: "I should have written to you before this, but for the unsettled life we have led since our arrival in Cuba

… Uncle spends two hours a day in the sugar house, the vapor of which is highly recommended in pulmonary affections."

While Buchanan may have been in denial about the seriousness of his friend's illness, William Sharkey was clearly alarmed by King's frailty. The Cuban Consul General wrote Secretary of State William Marcy there appeared to be "but little ground to hope for recovery."

King sensed he was nearing death's doorstep. In early April, he informed his niece that he wanted to spend his last days in Alabama. On April 8, soon after returning to Havana, the pair again boarded *The U.S.S. Fulton*. Four days later, the steamship docked in Mobile.

Southern historian Katharine Hopkins Chapman documented King's arrival in the port city: "A great throng was assembled on the wharf to greet the eminent statesman."

Chapman recalled crewmen physically supporting the critically ill Vice-President as he disembarked: "He appeared extremely feeble. But with head erect, he looked eagerly, sadly at his beloved Alabama."

King rested for a few days at Mobile's Battle House Hotel before boarding another steamer, *The Royal St. John*, for his final upriver journey home. He arrived at King's Bend on April 17 with little time to spare.

The following day, King remained completely bedbound, struggling to speak between labored breaths. At 6:00 p.m., on April 18, 1853, William Rufus de Vane King fulfilled his wish "to die in my own bed."

A family member present at his bedside recalled King's final words: "Hush let me pass quickly."

One day after returning home, 11 days before his 67th birthday, 25 days after being sworn into office, and seven years and 359 days before the first shots of the Civil War were fired, Alabama's first and only Vice-President died before he could return to Washington, D.C. and fulfill his sworn duties.

POSTLOGUE

In the days, weeks, and months following his death, King was eulogized by friends and colleagues throughout the country. Virginia Senator Robert Hunter introduced a resolution to both Houses of Congress allowing lawmakers to offer personal tributes to the deceased Vice-President.

"Here, at least, is a public man, in whose life there can be found no instance of a mean or equivocating action, none of the departure from the lofty sense of honor. ... Of all the public men I have known, there are none whose lives teach more impressively the great moral of strength of which public virtue gives than that of Colonel King. ... His political career may be said to have been one triumphant march through life, a march in which his step neither faltered nor stumbled, in ascending to that place, which was perhaps the chief object of his aspiration," Hunter proclaimed.

Massachusetts Senator Edward Everett praised King for his leadership skills, encyclopedic knowledge of parliamentary rules of order, and conciliatory nature: "I can say nothing but what is good of him, for I have never seen or heard anything but good of him for 30 years that I have known him personally and by reputation. ... He possessed in an eminent degree, that quickness of perception, that promptness of decision, that familiarity with the now somewhat complicated rules of Congressional proceedings, and urbanity of manner, which are required in a presiding officer. ... In fact, sir, he was highly endowed with what Cicero beautifully commands as the *boni Senatoris prudentia*, the "wisdom of a good Senator," and in his accurate study and ready application of the rules of parliamentary law, he rendered a service to the country, not perhaps of the brilliant kind, but assuredly of no secondary importance."

Michigan Senator Lewis Cass joined the chorus mourning the loss of an esteemed colleague: "The places that knew him will know him no more; but though dead, his memory is embalmed in the hearts of his countrymen, and there it will live, honored and cherished, long after all those who are now taking part of this tribute to his worth, shall have followed him in the journey, where for a brief space, he has preceded us through the dark valley of the shadow of death."

Illinois Senator Stephen Douglas, more often inclined to self-adulation than recognizing achievements of others, offered a praiseworthy eulogy before joint Houses of Congress: "Those whose happiness it was to be associated with Colonel King, in public duty and private intercourse, are alone capable of realizing the extent of our loss. His example in all the relations of life, public and private, may be safely commended to our children as worthy of imitation. Few men in this country have ever served the public for so long a period of time and a more fervent patriotism to command the confidence, admiration, and gratitude of an enlightened constituency. ... William R. King, as a brother Senator on this floor, during the greater part of that long period, I was an attentive observer of his course as a public man, and I cannot in justice remain silent when an opportunity is offered of paying a tribute to the memory of one who so honorably deserved it."

In addition to noble orations filling pages of *The Congressional Record*, King was symbolically honored. Flags were lowered to half-staff in Washington D.C. and throughout the state of Alabama. King's former seat in the Senate chambers was also draped in black.

On December 5, 1853, during his 1st Annual Message to Congress, delivered in writing, President Franklin Pierce offered a belated tribute to King: "Since the adjournment of Congress, the Vice-President of the United States has passed from the scenes of earth, without having entered upon the duties of the station to which he had been called by the voice of his countrymen. Having occupied, almost continuously, for more than 30 years, a seat in one or other of the two Houses of Congress, and having by his single purity and wisdom, secured unbounded confidence and universal respect, his failing health was watched by the nation with painful solitude. His loss to the country, under all circumstances, has been justly regarded as irreparable."

Article II, Section 3, Clause 1 of the United States Constitution, mandated the President "shall from time to time give to the Congress Information of the State of the Union, and recommend to their Consideration such measures as he shall judge necessary and expedient." But why did Pierce deliver his address in written form?

The nation's first two Presidents, George Washington and John Adams delivered their Annual Messages to Congress in person. Beginning in 1811, Adams' successor, Thomas Jefferson, who considered verbal addresses "monarchial" in nature, sent only written messages to Capitol Hill.

Jefferson's tradition remained in effect for the remainder of the 19th and early 20th Centuries, including Pierce's Administration. On December 2, 1913, Woodrow Wilson, 28th President of the United States, began delivering his annual addresses to Congress in person.

In 1935, Franklin Roosevelt became the first President to use the term State of the Union Address. After invention of the radio in 1923, it became common to broadcast the annual messages live throughout the country. In 1947, President Harry Truman delivered the first televised State of the Union Address.

In modern times, State of the Union Addresses occur in January of each year and are transmitted live to global audiences via radio, television, and the Internet. Presidents utilize the speeches to encourage lawmakers to support the Executive Branch's legislative agenda and convey their "vision" to the entire nation.

In the immediate aftermath of King's demise, James Buchanan

POSTLOGUE

remained ensconced in his Lancaster, Pennsylvania manor without offering a public eulogy honoring his long-time friend. He did, however, pen a few personal letters to their mutual friends. In a missive delivered to Francis Wilkinson Pickens, former Congressman and future Governor of South Carolina, Buchanan wrote he had "never known a purer or better man" than King. In the same letter, Buchanan acknowledged having lived with King "for many years as a brother," and characterized his deceased friend as an "aimable, kind-hearted, sound-judging, and consistent gentleman." Buchanan's reticence about issuing public statements may have been motivated, at least in part, by self-protection. Resurrection of past salacious rumors about the exact nature of his long-standing friendship with King could have damaged his future political ambitions.

King's funeral was held at St. John's Episcopal Church in Selma. Alabama Senator Arthur Bagby was among those eulogizing his friend and long-time public servant. Bagby proclaimed, "neither envy, nor hate, nor malice, nor any uncharitableness [sic] ever whispered a tale of dishonor against him or attempted to cast the slightest state of suspicion upon the spotless purity of his character."

As specified in his will, King was entombed in the family cemetery adjacent to his plantation home. King further specified the graveyard be named Piney Hills and house "large and airy vaults" capable of accommodating "10 or 12 bodies."

Unmarried and childless, King had composed his last will and testament on January 1, 1853, less than four months before his death. He left his King's Bend plantation and other land holdings to William Thomas King and Margaret William King, the son and daughter-in-law of his brother Thomas. The couple also inherited his dinnerware and silverware. King bequeathed a number of acres of Dallas County farmland to one of his sisters with the provision that she pass it along to her own daughter. Another sister inherited a plantation King owned in nearby Lowndes County.

At the time of his death, King owned 159 slaves. The slaves he most valued were bequeathed to various family members, but his heirs were forbidden from dividing families by selling slaves to different owners. In his will, King freed more than half of his slaves. Newly freed men, women, and children who wished to migrate to Liberia were compensated for travel expenses from designated funds in King's estate. Freed slaves were also permitted to relocate to non-slave states.

While King clearly spelled out in writing his wishes to be entombed in the Piney Hills family cemetery at King's Bend, civic leaders in Selma eventually decided his remains should be moved to a more austere location, easily accessible to the public. Many locals were also alarmed by Piney Hill's susceptibility to flooding following torrential downpours which caused the banks of the Alabama River to overflow.

From distant Pennsylvania, James Buchanan chimed in on the proposed relocation. He advised that his close friend's "remains, undoubtedly ought to be removed to Selma."

In 1882, the Selma City Council appointed a committee to select a new site for King's mausoleum. The process of relocating his body, however, was not lacking in drama.

Renowned Alabama author, Kathryn Windham, recounted the conflict in her book entitled *Alabama: One Big Family Porch*: "After the War Between the States and after the Reconstruction years that followed, some citizens of Selma began a movement to have King's body brought from its remote resting place to a more suitable shrine in the city he founded and named. King's body belonged in Selma, they said. City officials agreed with this line of reasoning, and so did many members of the King family, particularly the branch living in Tuscaloosa. The Dallas County branch mostly wanted to leave King's body at the spot he himself had chosen as his final resting place. Quite a family feud developed between the two factions, and some harsh words were exchanged."

Securing the body absent uniform consensus from King's

descendants led to a tomb-raiding expedition. According to one account, a Selma funeral home director, last name Breslin, traveled to King's Bend in the middle of the night accompanied by three other men. Lacking the key necessary to access to King's mausoleum, one of the men used a sledge hammer to destroy the lock. After the burial vault was opened, King's coffin was transferred to the bed of a mule-drawn wagon, concealed with strewn hay, and transported to Breslin's Undertaking Establishment in Selma.

The second story differs to some degree. The Mayor of Selma and a lone companion purloined King's remains under the cover of darkness and transported the coffin to Selma in a wagon. Perhaps an embellishment, some recall a gun battle ensued between the grave robbers and certain members of the King family. If shots were fired, no record of casualties exists.

While logistics of the transfer are debatable, King's remains were no doubt relocated to Selma 29 years after his death and entombed within the walls of a white marble mausoleum at Live Oak Cemetery. Amid live oak trees draped with Spanish moss, King's name and brief biographical information were engraved in stone above the entrance to his newly-constructed tomb.

A free-standing marker was later erected adjacent to the mausoleum, denoting King's lifetime accomplishments: "Native Sampson County, North Carolina. Admitted to bar, 1806. North Carolina House of Commons, 1807-1809. U.S. Congressman, 1811-1816. U.S. Legation Naples and St. Petersburg, 1816-1818. Moved to Dallas, County, Alabama, 1818. A founder of Selma; named city. Delegate to Alabama Constitutional Convention, 1819. U.S. Senator 1819-1844, 1848-1853. U.S. Minister to France, 1844-1846. President Pro Tempore U.S. Senate 1836-1840, 1850-1852. Vice-President of the United States, 1853."

King's Dallas County plantation home was destroyed by fire during the 1930s. The King's Bend plantation was later purchased by Buchanan Lumber Mobile, Inc. (Incidentally, the company's founder was not related to James Buchanan).

Selma, Alabama and surrounding areas are the final resting places for many 19th Century slave owners. More than a century after King's death, Selma was infamously introduced to the entire nation.

On Sunday, March 7, 1965, local law enforcement officers, Alabama State Troopers, and a civilian posse of white supremacists violently attacked hundreds of mostly Black civil rights marchers attempting to cross the Edmund Pettus Bridge spanning the Alabama River on downtown Selma's eastside. The assault victims were in the process of initiating a symbolic "March to Montgomery" protesting widespread, racially discriminatory voting registration policies in Dallas County. More than 15 marchers were hospitalized after inhaling tear gas and absorbing repeated blows from nightsticks and baseball bats. The brutal and unprovoked attacks, captured by television cameras from all three national networks, *CBS*, *NBC*, and *ABC*, were replayed in homes throughout the country. Most Americans were appalled by the brutal events occurring on what will forever be remembered as "Bloody Sunday."

Federal District Court Judge Frank M. Johnson, Jr. soon issued an affirmative injunction allowing a peaceful march to proceed (to learn more about the iconic Johnson, please refer the author's book, *You Were Right and We Were Wrong*). Afterwards, Civil Rights leader Martin Luther King, Jr. led a peaceful march from Selma to Alabama's capital city. Beginning on March 25, 1965, thousands of demonstrators, including local Black citizens, members of the Southern Christian Leadership Conference (SCLC) and the Student Nonviolent Coordinating Committee (SNCC), as well as enthusiastic, progressive-minded whites began walking along the highway leading to Montgomery. Throughout the five-day, 54-mile trek, marchers were protected from further assaults by 1,000 military policemen and 2,000 U.S. Army troops. The march concluded adjacent to Alabama's State Capitol Building, where Dr. King delivered a rousing speech devoted to African Americans' unrelenting quest to achieve equal rights in Alabama and the rest of the country.

"The end we seek is a society at peace with itself, a society that can live with its conscience," King proclaimed in his booming but melodic cadence. (Segregationist Governor George C. Wallace, peeking through window blinds in his office suite, was amazed by the number of Freedom Marchers congregated at the base of State Capitol Building steps).

Appalled by brutality of Bloody Sunday, President Lyndon B. Johnson introduced the Voting Rights Act of 1965. Having shepherded passage of the Civil Rights Act a year earlier, Johnson originally planned to wait until at least 1966 before addressing racially discriminatory voting practices, in order to give Southern segregationist lawmakers a "cooling off" period.

After the horror of Bloody Sunday, Johnson concluded immediate action was necessary to address Black disenfranchisement. In one of the most passionate and prosaic addresses of his legendary career, the President introduced a voting rights bill to a joint session of Congress. After Congressional approval, Johnson signed the Civil Rights Act of 1965 into law on August 6, 1965. A century after conclusion of the Civil War, Blacks throughout Alabama were finally granted Constitutionally-mandated access to polling places originally proscribed by the 15th Amendment to the U.S. Constitution.

Compared to many 19th Century statesmen, including Henry Clay, Daniel Webster, and John Quincy Adams, the life and times of William Rufus de Vane King have not been as extensively chronicled or memorialized. Nonetheless, his name has not been entirely forgotten.

A county in Virginia bears his name. In 1852, the Oregon Territorial Legislature christened King County in honor of his crucial role in establishing the Oregon and Washington Territories during 19th Century westward migration of settlers. The county remained his namesake after the Washington Territory was carved out and admitted to the Union as the 42nd state in 1889. On April 19, 2005, however,

Washington Governor Christine Gregoire signed into law Senate Bill 532. Beginning on July 24 that year, the county was re-dedicated in honor of Martin Luther King, Jr. The Governor and State Legislature concluded King County would permanently bear the name of an iconic civil rights leader rather than an Antebellum-era slaveholder.

Seattle, Washington's Kingdome, officially opened on March 27, 1976 (and was imploded on March 26, 2000), prior to Senate Bill 532 becoming law, and the county still bore William R. King's name. During the Kingdome's 24-year existence, the facility was home to the National Football League's Seattle Seahawks, Major League Baseball's Seattle Mariners, and the now defunct National Basketball Association's Seattle Supersonics. The indoor stadium also hosted other professional and intercollegiate sporting events as well as numerous high-profile musical concerts and various conventions.

King is well-remembered in his birth state. A bronze bust of the statesman, sculpted by Karl Gruppe and funded by Congress in 1930, stands atop a granite base outside the Sampson County Courthouse in Clinton, North Carolina. A student dormitory at the University of North Carolina bears King's name. In 1988, the thoroughfare between Newton and Clinton, North Carolina was formally designated William Rufus King Road. A historical marker honoring King was erected at the corner of U.S. Highway 701 and State Road 1845 in Newton Grove, North Carolina.

King's memory lingers in the nation's capital. In 1896, a marble bust sculpted by William C. McCauslen was added to the U.S. Senate's Vice-Presidential collection.

The 13th Vice-President has also been honored in his adopted state of Alabama. Portraits of King are displayed in the Selma-Dallas County Public Library and Selma's Vaughn-Smitherman Museum. The Alabama Department of Archives in Montgomery houses the William Rufus King Room. In 1953, a group of Alabamians traveled to Cuba and erected a historic marker at Matanzas where King was sworn in office as Vice-President a century earlier.

POSTLOGUE

Less than six months after King's death, his close friend James Buchanan emerged from self-proclaimed retirement when President Franklin Pierce appointed him American Foreign Minister to the Court of St. James. At that point in history, aside from serving as a Cabinet officer, Foreign Minister to Great Britain was regarded as the most prestigious position in federal government. Buchanan, whose political resume was quite extensive, initially appeared unimpressed by the President's offer. As might have been expected, Buchanan was paralyzed by indecision, changing his mind twice before accepting the ministership.

In August 1853, Buchanan boarded a steamship, *The Atlantic*, bound for the United Kingdom. Harriet Lane accompanied her bachelor uncle to England and served as his official hostess during diplomatic receptions and formal dinners. After arriving in London, Buchanan and Lane occupied the American Minister's stately residence at 56 Hartley Street in Cavendish Square.

Attractive and vivacious, Lane attracted the eye of many suitors. Impressed by her poise, grace, and beauty, Queen Victoria expressed hope Lane would wed an Englishman and make the mother country her permanent home. No doubt flirtatious, Lane never married a Brit.

While living abroad, Buchanan kept a close eye on the American political scene. However, he refrained from issuing public opinions about the escalating sectional controversy over slavery for fear of jeopardizing his long-standing Presidential aspirations.

Meanwhile, the Kansas-Nebraska Act, drafted in large part by Illinois Democratic Senator Stephen Douglas, yet another Presidential aspirant, pushed America closer to outright civil war. Passed by Congress in May 1854 and signed into law by President Pierce shortly thereafter, the measure divided the existing Nebraska Territory; one portion retained its original name while the second was christened the Kansas Territory.

The Kansas-Nebraska Act ended latitudinal demarcation separating free and slave states, rendering the Missouri Compromise of 1820 null and void. From that point forward, voters in all territories, regardless of geographical location, would determine the legality of slavery by popular sovereignty.

Following the enactment of the Kansas-Nebraska Act, the Whig Party was swept into the ash bin of history, unable to maintain a working alliance between pro- and anti-slavery members. Many former Whigs joined the Free Soil Party or the short-lived but influential American Party. The latter group were commonly referred to as "Know Nothings." Required to renounce Catholicism and adopt restrictive, religiously biased immigration policies, party members were secretly instructed to reply, "I know nothing," when questioned by outsiders. Despite winning numerous elections on state and national levels, the Know Nothings were unable to sustain a lengthy existence based almost exclusively on their uncompromising prejudicial agenda.

Many ex-Whigs and Free Soilers eventually found a permanent home in the country's first-ever, anti-slavery party, the Republicans. The Republican Party was formally established in Ripon, Wisconsin, on March 20, 1854. Unlike Know Nothings and Free Soilers, the Republican Party proved long-lasting and formidable.

All the while, Buchanan remained a comfortable distance away from domestic political fray and was not forced to take a public stance concerning the legality and morality of the controversial Kansas-Nebraska Act. Doughfaced Buchanan, however, remained no less committed to protecting interests of Southern slaveholders.

In May 1854, he outlined his neutral position in a letter to a fellow Pennsylvanian: "I have no opinion to any person on the Nebraska Bill. I have thought in a foreign land & with a desire to part from public life in peace with all friends, I might be justified in my silence."

While serving as Minister to the Court of St. James, Buchanan failed to negotiate any major compromises beneficial to the United States. He was unable to convince the British government to abandon the Bay Islands off the coast of Honduras, withdraw from mahogany-rich

Belize, or relinquish protectorate status over Mosquito (also known as Moskito) Island in the Caribbean.

Buchanan's most ambitious and pseudo-diplomatic proposal ended in embarrassing failure. Consumed by Manifest Destiny, he believed America possessed the divine right to acquire Cuba by any means necessary. The island nation, just 90 miles from Florida's southernmost shore, was covered by rich layers of soil conducive to large-scale cotton cultivation.

Collaborating with Pierre Soule, American Minister to Spain, and John Mason, American Minister to France, Buchanan drafted the Ostend Manifesto, named for the Belgian city where the proposal originated. Based on the document's language style alone, many of Buchanan's contemporaries concluded he was the primary author of the controversial measure.

The Ostend Manifesto proposed Spain, without prior consultation, would sell Cuba to the United State for $100,000,000. Buchanan assumed Spain, beset with financial difficulties amid the throes of revolution, was eager to shed Cuba for the right price. In conjunction with Soule and Mason, Buchanan further concluded America had every right to *seize* Cuba if Spain refused to sell its distant colony.

"We shall be justified in wresting Cuba from Spain," Buchanan boldly asserted, echoing the tenets of Manifest Destiny.

On the home front, however, Buchanan's proposal encountered a road block. Secretary of State William L. Marcy, a New Yorker who also harbored Presidential ambitions, was unwilling to back any measure alienating Northern anti-slavery voters. As a high-ranking Cabinet officer, Marcy convinced President Pierce to reject the Ostend Manifesto.

Buchanan's ambitious plan to add Cuba as a pro-slavery home for affluent Southern cotton planters died on the vine. Many historians regard the proposal to take possession of Cuba by purchase or force as one of the worst miscalculations of Buchanan's lengthy career as a public servant.

While living in Europe, Buchanan feigned disinterest in the 1856 Presidential election. In reality, his ambitions were aflame.

"In the beginning, I did all I could to prevent any movement in my favor and what has since been done has been entirely spontaneous, at least as far as I am concerned," he disingenuously wrote a friend in February 1856.

Buchanan completed his service as Foreign Minister in the spring of 1856 and returned home aboard *The Atlantic*, the same steamship that transported him to England nearly three years earlier. By the time he reached homeland, Buchanan was clearly regarded as a leading candidate for the Democratic Presidential nomination. So-called "Wheatland Clubs," named after Buchanan's Pennsylvania estate, were actively forming throughout the country. Wheatlanders proclaimed Buchanan was the most experienced and least controversial potential nominee heading into the 1856 Democratic National Convention. When Buchanan returned to Pennsylvania, the Lancaster Wheatland Club fired a congratulatory homecoming salute from a cannon nicknamed "Old Buck."

Buchanan was cautiously optimistic, fully aware he had been denied the Democratic Presidential nomination on three previous occasions. At age 65, Buchanan believed 1856 would represent his final opportunity to grasp the elusive brass ring.

In June, the Democratic National Convention opened in Cincinnati, Ohio, the first time in history a national party convened outside one of America's original 13 states. While he lacked universal personal and political appeal, Buchanan's critics could not ignore his impressive record of public service in the Legislative and Executive branches of government. Aware he was supported by many Conservative Northern and Southern Democrats, party operatives deemed Buchanan the *safest* choice among proposed Presidential nominees.

While Buchanan's popularity with Northern voters was never uniform, Southern Democrats were aware the doughface supported both the legality of slavery and the right to expand the institution into western territories. At the same time, Buchanan's self-proclaimed personal hatred of slavery was enough to mollify a minority bloc of Democratic Abolitionists. (The vast majority of Abolitionists now identified as

Republicans).

Buchanan's chief rivals for the nomination included incumbent President Franklin Pierce, Illinois Senator Stephen Douglas (primary author of the controversial Kansas-Nebraska Act), and Michigan Senator Lewis Cass. After 14 deadlocked ballots, Pierce withdrew from the contest. Three ballots later, a delighted Buchanan won the long-coveted nomination.

Kentucky Congressman John C. Breckinridge was subsequently nominated as Buchanan's running mate. While Kentucky was considered more of a Border than Southern state, it was nonetheless a locale where slavery was legal. Consequently, Breckinridge brought crucial regional balance to the Democratic ticket. (Breckinridge would unsuccessfully run for President in 1860 as the nominee of the National Democratic Party, one of three coalitions formed after the traditional Democratic Party fragmented over disagreements concerning Slave Codes. He was later appointed Secretary of War for the Confederate States of America during the final fateful months of the Civil War).

In June 1856, Republicans nominated 43-year-old John C. Fremont as the party's *first-ever Presidential candidate*. Dark-haired, bearded, and handsome, Fremont first made a name for himself by exploring modern day California, Oregon, and Nevada. The aptly named "Pathfinder" was also a decorated U.S. Army officer who fought in the Mexican-American War, served as Governor of the California Territory, and was elected as one of the Golden State's first U.S. Senators. Former New Jersey Senator William L. Dayton was nominated as Fremont's running mate.

The active but now less influential Know Nothing Party, bound by Protestant piety and prejudice, nominated former President Millard Fillmore to run for President. Convention delegates selected Andrew Jackson Donelson, one-time Democrat and adopted son of famed Old Hickory, as Fillmore's running mate.

In that era, few Presidential candidates actively participated on the campaign trail. While Buchanan ran a "front porch" race from his home in Pennsylvania, Democratic political operatives, also known as

"Buchaneers," canvassed the country on his behalf.

The Grand National Democratic Banner featured pictures of Buchanan and Breckinridge captioned with the slogan: "ONE COUNTRY, ONE CONSTITUTION, ONE DESTINY."

On Election Day 1856, 79.4 percent of the electorate cast Presidential ballots. After the votes were tallied, Buchanan emerged triumphant, winning 45.28 percent of the popular vote and accumulating 174 electoral votes. At age 35, Breckinridge became America's youngest Vice-President Elect.

Fremont won 33.1 percent of the popular vote and 114 electoral votes. Fillmore finished a distant third—21.5 percent of the vote but accumulated only eight electoral votes.

Buchanan clearly owed his victory to pro-slavery voters. He carried all Southern and Border States except for Maryland (won by Fillmore). In sharp contrast, Buchanan won only 4 of 14 Northern states. In his home state of Pennsylvania, Buchanan's margin of victory was only 3,000 votes out of 423,000 cast. The new President was no doubt beholden to the South for achieving his cherished goal.

"Mr. Buchanan and the Northern Democracy are dependent upon the South," a Virginia Judge affirmed.

Election of a Northern President loathe to disappoint Southern slaveholders was a recipe for disaster. In the final years leading up to the Civil War, the ineffectual doughface was in an untenable position. Buchanan's assertions that secession was unconstitutional but slavery itself was a right guaranteed by American's founding fathers proved irreconcilable.

On March 4, 1857, Buchanan was inaugurated as the 15th President of the United States. Under sunny skies accompanied by mild temperatures, the largest ever Inauguration Day crowd witnessed the oath of office ceremony. Unbeknownst to Buchanan, assumption of power would be the high point of his much-maligned Presidency.

Just three days after Buchanan took office, the U.S. Supreme Court issued its much-anticipated ruling in the case of *Dred Scott v. Sanford*. By a 6-3 margin, the high court declared slaves were *not American citizens* and had no legal right to sue for freedom from bondage.

Seventy-nine-year-old Chief Justice Roger Taney, a native of Maryland and former slave owner, not only wrote the majority opinion but also penned a controversial *obiter dictum*. *Obiter dictum* is a Latin term for statements that are neither central to a given case nor legally binding.

At this point in history, Taney had served on the Supreme Court for 22 years, and his tenure as Chief Justice was the second longest of any high court jurist. (Only John Marshall, Chief Justice from 1801-35, had exceeded Taney's length of service).

In his *obiter dictum*, Taney proclaimed Congress had no power to exclude slavery from any territory, thereby rendering the Missouri Compromise unconstitutional. The compromise bill, passed by Congress in 1820 and signed into law by President James Monroe, had banned slavery north of America's 36-degree, 30-minute latitude, excepting the Missouri Territory. (Congress had earlier negated the Missouri Compromise by passing the Kansas-Nebraska Act).

Taney further opined Blacks were "beings of an inferior order" and held "no rights which any white man was bound to respect." The Chief Justice also declared slaves were *private property* and their ownership by white masters was protected by the due process clause of the 5th Amendment.

Buchanan's unqualified endorsement of the controversial Supreme Court ruling immediately alienated him from *all* Americans who opposed slavery. The President was further rebuffed when Congress failed to approve the Kansas Territory's Lecompton Constitution. (Pro- and anti-slavers had established separate territorial capital cities, Lecompton and Topeka). The document, approved by a *minority* of territorial voters but nonetheless supported by Buchanan, would have eventually resulted in Kansas' admission to the Union as a slave state. Lawmakers, however, refused to accept a Constitution that failed to represent the wishes of a majority of the territory's voters. (Kansas was eventually admitted the Union as a free state on January 29, 1861, the final lame duck months of Buchanan's single term as President)

Buchanan's popularity and influence continued to plummet. In the 1858 mid-term elections, anti-slavery Republicans won a majority of Northern Congressional and Gubernatorial races. In the House of Representatives alone, anti-slavers gained 22 seats. Just four years after the party's birth, Republicans accounted for 40 percent of the House's membership. For the remaining two years of his ineffectual Administration, Buchanan found it difficult to establish collaborative relationships with lawmakers.

The Financial Panic of 1857 also occurred on Buchanan's watch. In August of that year, the collapse of the Ohio Life and Trust Bank initiated a devastating ripple effect. Nationwide, more than 1,400 financial institutions failed and over 5,000 business owners eventually declared bankruptcy.

Buchanan's response was much like President Van Buren's during the Financial Panic of 1837. Blaming the crisis on greedy speculators, he refused to stimulate the economy by investing in government-funded public works projects. In his Annual Message to Congress, the President proclaimed the federal government "was without power to extend relief." (In fairness to Van Buren and Buchanan, many modern-day economists argue federal spending during depressions and recessions, while offering hope to the unemployed, fails to remedy financial crises).

Buchanan made powerful and unneeded enemies in business and financial sectors by directly attacking investors and bankers. While Presidents are not solely responsible for the country's financial stability, by the end of Buchanan's four years in office, the federal government's budget surplus had been transformed into a $1,200,000 deficit.

Buchanan's Administration was also tainted by allegations of corruption. Several of his appointees were accused of engaging in financial improprieties. While Buchanan was not guilty of committing illegal acts, underlings likely accepted monetary kickbacks, awarded government contracts to political allies rather than low bidders, and misappropriated public funds for personal use.

Prior to the 1860 Presidential election, aware his prospects for re-election were zero, Buchanan made no effort to secure the Democratic nomination. After Abraham Lincoln was elected as the nation's first Republican President, Southern planters were convinced he planned to immediately abolish slavery and destroy their labor-intensive agrarian society. (In reality, early in his Presidency, Lincoln's goal was to prevent further expansion of slavery but not abolishment in states where the institute was already legal. In fact, Lincoln still supported proposals to colonize slaves outside the United States. As the bloody Civil War progressed, he revised his plans. On January 1, 1863, President Lincoln issued the Emancipation Proclamation, declaring "that all persons held as slaves" living within rebellious Confederate states "are, and henceforward, shall be free."

Southern Democrats, however, were firmly convinced the newly elected President was a "Black Republican" Abolitionist. Consequently, on December 20, 1860, roughly six weeks after Lincoln's election, South Carolina became the first state to secede from the Union. Over the next six weeks, Mississippi, Florida, Alabama, Georgia, Louisiana, and Texas followed suit. As winter transitioned to spring, Virginia, North Carolina, Tennessee, and Arkansas joined the secessionist wave.

After the 1860 Presidential election, Buchanan was the lamest of ducks. Acknowledging secession was unconstitutional, Buchanan muddied the waters by declaring the President was powerless to halt disunion. His contradictory statements and paralyzing indecisiveness confused and angered Union loyalists.

In February 1861, delegates from the seceded Southern states convened in Montgomery, Alabama and formally birthed a new nation, the Confederate States of America (CSA). Convention delegates elected former Mississippi Senator Jefferson Davis President of the CSA and one time Georgia Congressman, Alexander H. Stephens, as his fire-eating Vice-President.

The Confederate states, eventually numbering 11, were directed to seize all federal assets within their respective borders, including forts and arsenals. Buchanan made only one effort to intervene, an unsuccessful attempt to reinforce South Carolina's Fort Sumter with much-needed provisions. After Buchanan dispatched a steam-powered merchant ship, *The Star of the West*, laden with foodstuff, clothing, and other staples, absent troops, weapons, or ammunition, South Carolina militiamen unleashed a barrage of artillery fire, forcing the unarmed vessel to beat a hasty retreat before reaching Charleston Harbor's Fort Sumter.

In the final tumultuous weeks of his Administration, Buchanan was on the brink of total physical and mental breakdown. On March 4, 1861, the day Abraham Lincoln was inaugurated as the 16th President of the United States, a haggard Buchanan was more than eager to relinquish the office.

"If you are as happy in entering the White House as I shall feel returning to Wheatland, you are a happy man," Buchanan informed his successor as they stood side-by-side on the steps of the U.S. Capitol Building.

Less than six weeks after Lincoln's inauguration, South Carolina militiamen opened fire on Fort Sumter itself, forcing surrender of the island fortress and igniting the American Civil War. Over the next four years, 600,000 individuals, *2.5 percent* of the nation's population, would die from battlefield wounds or rampant, close-quarter spread of infectious diseases.

Post-Presidency, Buchanan permanently retired from elective office and returned to his Pennsylvania home. After the Union emerged victorious in the Civil War, ratification of the 13th Amendment abolished slavery. The 14th and 15th Amendments granted equal rights and suffrage to Black Americans. (While slavery was immediately abolished, a century would pass before racial discrimination in public accommodations and polling booths, particularly in the Deep South, were halted by the federal government, ending the shameful era of Jim Crow rule).

For the remainder of his life, Buchanan remained an unrepentant doughface, far more invested in maintaining States' Rights than enforcing civil rights. The ex-President opposed universal Black suffrage, arguing voter eligibility requirements should be decided by individual states.

POSTLOGUE

On June 1, 1868, just over three years after the Civil War ended, 77-year-old James Buchanan died of pneumonia in his second-story bedroom. The 15th President of the United States was laid to rest in Lancaster's Woodward Hill Cemetery.

Many historians and presidential biographers rate Buchanan's Administration as the most ineffectual in American history. After achieving his cherished goal of being elected President, the outcome proved disastrous.

William R. King was also elected to his dream office. But his death only 25 days after being sworn into office as Vice-President shielded King from the secessionist crisis, four years of Civil War bloodshed, and the tumultuous era of Reconstruction.

Unlike Buchanan, King's reputation as statesman and conciliator were preserved, at least in part, by the timing of his death.

AFTERWORD

William Rufus de Vane King was a public servant on state, federal, and international levels for most of his adult life. In his birth state, the young lawyer first served in the North Carolina House of Commons. At the tender age of 25, King was elected to the U.S. House of Representatives. After serving as a Congressman for more than five years, he traveled to Europe in the role of Legation Secretary to the American Minister to modern day Italy and Russia.

After migrating to the Alabama Territory's Black Belt region in 1818, King established firm roots as an affluent member of the Antebellum-era cotton planter class. The timing of his relocation also proved politically fortuitous. King was elected as a delegate to the territory's Constitutional Convention, the final step enabling Alabama to become the 22nd state admitted to the Union. After serving on the committee responsible for drafting the Constitution, King was elected one of Alabama's first two U.S. Senators.

On Capitol Hill, King earned respect from fellow lawmakers for his work ethic, congeniality, conciliatory skills, and encyclopedic knowledge of parliamentary rules. King's colleagues eventually elected him President Pro-Tempore of the Senate, where he served from 1836-40.

After King served more than two decades in the U.S. Senate, President John Tyler appointed him American Minister to France.

AFTERWORD

During his two years as a diplomat, King fulfilled his assignment with flying colors, convincing the French government to refrain from allying with England in attempts to prevent America's annexation of the Republic of Texas and providing Mexico with military aid during the war to come. In 1848, after returning to America, King was again elected to the U.S. Senate by the Alabama State Legislature, where he served an additional four years. During his second stint in the Senate, King's colleagues once again elected him President Pro Tempore (1850-52).

In November 1852, King fulfilled his dream of being elected Vice-President of the United States. Suffering from active tuberculosis, he was unable to actively participate in the Presidential campaign. After resigning from the Senate, the Vice-President Elect traveled to Cuba, hoping the island country's climate and salt air would slow progression of his deadly illness.

King's poor health prevented him from returning to Washington, D.C. on Inauguration Day. After Congressional approval, on March 4, 1853, King became the only President or Vice-President in American history to be sworn into office on foreign soil.

Terminally ill, King returned to Alabama in April of that year. Arriving at his plantation home with little time to spare, King died the following day. Serving as Vice-President for only 25 days, King is one of seven men who have died after being elected to the office.

In addition to King, Vice-Presidents George Clinton and Elbridge Gerry expired while in office during James Madison's two terms as President. Henry Wilson (Ulysess S. Grant), Thomas Hendricks (Grover Cleveland), Garet Hobart (William McKinley), and James Sherman (William Howard Taft) round out the list of Vice-Presidents who died before completing their terms. Two others, John C. Calhoun (Andrew Jackson) and Spiro Agnew (Richard Nixon), resigned from office under clouds of controversy. To date, the office of Vice-President of the United States has stood vacant for nearly four decades due to deaths and resignations.

To date, eight of 46 individuals elected President have died before completing their terms. Four were murdered, beginning with Abraham

Lincoln, who died on April 15, 1861, less than 12 hours after actor-turned-assassin John Wilkes Booth shot him in the back of the head at Washington D.C.'s Ford's Theater.

On September 19, 1881, James A. Garfield died from complications of a gunshot wound to his back inflicted by Charles Julius Guiteau. On July 2 of that year, Guiteau shot the President at the Baltimore and Potomac Railroad Station in Washington, D.C.

William McKinley died eight days after Leon Frank Czolgosz shot him in the abdomen. On September 6, 1901, while the President was attending the Pan-American Exposition in Buffalo, New York, Czolgosz shot McKinley at point-blank range.

On November 22, 1963, John F. Kennedy was pronounced dead approximately 30 minutes after he was shot in the head by Lee Harvey Oswald. The assassin shot Kennedy during a Presidential motorcade in Dallas, Texas. (To learn more about America's presidential assassinations, please refer to the author's prior publications, *Rendezvous in Dallas and The Presidential Assassins*).

Four Presidents have died in office due to natural causes: William Henry Harrison from pneumonia on April 4, 1841, Zachary Taylor due to a gastrointestinal infection on July 9, 1850, Warren G. Harding from a heart attack on August 2, 1923, and Franklin D. Roosevelt from an acute brain hemorrhage on April 12, 1945.

To date, Richard M. Nixon is the only President to have resigned from office. Facing likely impeachment and criminal charges related to the infamous Watergate scandal, Nixon resigned on August 9, 1974.

On three separate occasions, William R. King found himself only a heartbeat away from the Presidency. After the deaths of Presidents Harrison and Taylor, President Pro Tempore King was next in line of succession after John Tyler and Millard Fillmore ascended to the Presidency following the unexpected demise of their predecessors. During his 25-day tenure as Vice-President, a sickly King was first in line to succeed President Pierce.

AFTERWORD

❧

In addition to his lengthy career as a public servant, King was a lawyer and affluent slaveholding planter in both his North Carolina birth state and adopted Alabama home. At the time of his death, King owned more than 150 slaves. At one point, the entire King family, including brothers, sisters, and other relatives, were the largest slaveholders in the state of Alabama.

An active participant in an institution that forever stained the moral fiber of the self-proclaimed "land of the free," King believed slavery was not only protected by the U.S. Constitution but also indispensable in an agrarian-based economy, heavily dependent upon human labor. At the same time, King was never a fire-eating secessionist, hell bent on fragmenting the country. As both a Southern Unionist and slaveholder, King was a political anomaly in the Deep South.

As a U.S. Senator, King was a conciliator of opinion and facilitator of the fragile alliance between America's pro- and anti-slavery proponents. As a Unionist, King's attempts to avert civil war were more often more respected and appreciated by his Northern colleagues than fellow Southern Democrats.

❧

By the time King was nominated to run for Vice-President in July 1852, he had spent more than 28 years in the United States Senate. At the time, his tenure was the second longest in American history.

King is the lone Vice-President of the United States to hail from the state of Alabama. He is also the state's *highest elected official*. Afflicted by terminal illness, King remains the only Vice-President who did not to live long enough to return to Washington, D.C. and fulfill his duties of office.

When researching and writing historical narratives, the author is often questioned about the subject of his forthcoming book. When the name William R. King was introduced into the conversation, the follow-up questions typically fell into one of two categories. Who was King? Was he the guy who was James Buchanan's gay lover?

King's life and times have been documented in previous pages, addressing the first question. The most accurate answer to the second inquiry is open to interpretation and of little importance to the historical record.

From an objective and well-studied point of view, King's sexual orientation is nothing more than a matter of speculation. Nonetheless, many students of history have repeatedly and decisively opined King and Buchanan were gay. Since there were no known witnesses to activities occurring behind either man's bedroom door, their sexual proclivities remain conjecture. Truthfully, King may have been heterosexual, gay, bisexual, or asexual.

Surviving private correspondence between King and Buchanan is decidedly one-sided, offering no definitive clues about the specifics of their long-time friendship. Some historians have mistakenly alleged their respective nieces, Catherine Margaret Ellis and Harriet Lane Johnston, destroyed *all private correspondence* exchanged between their uncles after King and Buchanan died.

Ellis and Lane have been accused of blindly following orders from their uncles to destroy private mutual correspondence for the express purpose of withholding details about their alleged intimate relationship. The disappearance of private letters, however, is only partly accurate.

In the late stages of Buchanan's life, Johnston assumed responsibility for organizing and characterizing her uncle's private and personal correspondence. In 1868, Johnston wrote Ellis to inform her of Buchanan's death and ask for return of any original letters exchanged

AFTERWORD

between King and her uncle for purposes of establishing a comprehensive and accurate biographical record.

Ellis wrote back offering her condolences and sharing fond remembrances of visiting Buchanan's Pennsylvania home: "I often transport myself to Wheatland, as it was and is."

In the same letter, Ellis informed Johnston she was uncertain about the status of her uncle's personal and private correspondence, supposedly left behind at his plantation home following King's death 15 years earlier: "There was at King's Bend a large package of letters from Mr. Buchanan to my Uncle, and I hope they may not have been destroyed in the commotion which was made of the place at surrender."

The "commotion" Ellis referred to, the Battle of Selma, was fought on April 2, 1865, just seven days before General Robert E. Lee surrendered Confederate forces under his command to Union General Ulysses S. Grant at Appomattox, Virginia, effectively ending the Civil War. By this point in time, all Confederate forces were on the verge of capitulation.

In the truest sense of the word, the skirmishes that occurred in and around Selma were hardly battles. By this point in the war, Confederate Army manpower was limited and widely dispersed. Consequently, a disproportionally small, rag-tag band of graycoats and local civilians, many of whom were older men and teenage boys, offered feeble defense against the siege of Selma's ironworks by experienced and well-armed Union Army soldiers. During the Battle of Selma, bluecoats burned the contents of many area plantation homes, if not the entire structures. Consequently, flames may have consumed much of King's correspondence.

"Among my souvenirs, I have two, or three, letters given to me by cousin, and which belonged to the package above named," Ellis further wrote.

None of the missives in Ellis' possession, however, were penned by Buchanan. Ellis promised Johnston she would contact Evelyn Hewett Collier King, widow of her cousin William Thomas King, hoping to learn additional details about existing letters to and from their uncles.

No such letters were known to have been recovered and any correspondence between the nieces related to this issue apparently ceased.

King and Buchanan undoubtedly exercised caution when exchanging missives. Some envelopes containing personal correspondence were marked "private" by one or the other. King and Buchanan were also known to request their letters be read and burned.

"Do not condemn this long letter to flames without reading it," King wrote on one occasion. (This missive, later discovered in Buchanan's private correspondence, proved it was never burned).

In 1846, King wrote Buchanan: "I read your kind letter attentively and then committed it to the flames as you requested."

"Your letter is in ashes," King penned in the postscript of a return letter dated 1852.

The paucity of surviving letters written by Buchanan to King suggests the latter was more faithful in following his friend's directions concerning destruction of incoming correspondence. Furthermore, Buchanan never wrote as many letters to King as he received in return.

Undelivered letters written to King were later discovered in Buchanan's personal papers. In March 1853, while King was in Cuba receiving treatment for tuberculosis, Buchanan asked a friend, William K. King, no relation to William R. King, to destroy a letter he (Buchanan) composed to the Vice-President-Elect.

"The letter to Mr. K has been disposed of according to your direction," William W. King informed Buchanan.

It is uncertain why Buchanan asked a third party to destroy a self-composed letter. But many of Buchanan's actions and inactions have long-defied understanding.

The fate of the "large packet of letters" once stored at King's plantation home remains unknown. There is no evidence Catherine Margaret Ellis located the correspondence in question. Harriet Lane Johnston provided the National Archives with two volumes of her uncle's papers in the 1880s. In addition, she assisted with publication of a 12-volume collection of his public and personal documents in the early 1900s. Neither work contains *any letters* written by Buchanan and delivered

AFTERWORD

to King.

George Ticknor Curtis, who penned one of the earliest biographies of the 15th President of the United States, included six letters composed by King to Buchanan, but *none* in reverse. The same can be said of Buchanan biographers William Reed and John Cadwalader. The six missives, none particularly intimate in nature, are housed at the Historical Society of Pennsylvania.

If King did keep any letters he received from Buchanan, the documents could have been burned by Union Army soldiers during the Battle of Selma, ruined by natural disaster, or mistakenly discarded by family members. On three occasions after King's death, flood waters from the Alabama River at least partially submerged what remained of his plantation home. It is also remotely possible that a portion of King's documents were stored in a New York City warehouse that burned in the late 1890s.

Some of King's papers, excluding letters from Buchanan, have survived. The largest collection is housed at the Alabama Department of Archives and History in Montgomery. However, only one box contains personal correspondence.

The remainder of King's existing personal and professional paper trail is limited and scattered: a single letter at the Boston Public Library, one letter and a photograph at the U.S. Library of Congress, a small scrapbook at the Maine Historical Society, one document at the Pierpont Morgan Library in New York City, and two letters in the Southern Historical Collection at the University of North Carolina. None of the private correspondence remotely hints at a sexual relationship with Buchanan.

As of today, more than 60 letters written from King to Buchanan still exist. The lack of correspondence addressed from Buchanan to King could easily be explained by the recipient's decision to destroy those letters. If King burned private letters from Buchanan, he may have strictly followed the sender's instructions or did so of his own volition. However, there is no evidence Ellis or Lane destroyed mutual correspondence between their uncles to cover up details about an alleged sexual relationship between King and Buchanan.

The two nieces remained friends for life. On one occasion, Ellis met Johnson who was vacationing in Cape May, New Jersey. During the reunion, Ellis met several of Buchanan's extended family members, including James Buchanan Johnston, great-nephew of the late statesman.

As she grew older, Ellis' mounting health problems and financial difficulties limited her ability to travel. Catherine Margaret Ellis, William R. King's niece, travel companion, and closest familial confidant, died in 1890 at her home in Camden, Alabama.

Johnstone endured her own series of hardships. Between 1881 and 1884, both of her children died from rheumatic fever and her husband succumbed to pneumonia. Coping with profound grief, Johnston toured Europe for a time. She later shared a townhome in Washington, D.C. with her cousin, May Kennedy.

Catherine Margaret Ellis, James Buchanan's loyal niece and White House hostess, died on July 3, 1903, at Narragansett Pier, Rhode Island. She was laid to rest next to her husband and children at Green Mount Cemetery in Baltimore. (Presidential assassin John Wilkes Booth and philanthropist Johns Hopkins are among historical figures buried at Green Mount, one of America's first garden cemeteries).

More than 171 years have passed since the death of William R. King. Since that time, a growing number of amateur and professional historians have spent considerable time focusing on his relationship with James Buchanan. Some researchers are unwavering in their opinions, while others offer measured analyses.

In November 1987, *Penthouse* magazine published an article written by Sharon Churcher, a British tabloid journalist. Tucked amid photographs of nude women, Churcher's biopic piece on James Buchanan was brazenly entitled, *Our First Gay President, Out of the Closet, Finally*.

AFTERWORD

As recently as 2010, Selma, Alabama lawyer J. L. Chestnutt was quoted in a newspaper article published by *The Tuscaloosa News*: "I don't think there's any question that King was a closet gay person. That is why Andrew Jackson called him 'Miss Nancy' and why others mocked him. ... I suspect if the truth had ever been known about King during his lifetime, he would not have achieved one-third of his splendid accomplishments on behalf of this nation."

Even the U.S. Senate Historical office dances around the issue of sexual proclivity: "King and Buchanan—both lifelong bachelors—became known as the 'Siamese twins'."

Other noted authors have described the relationship between King and Buchanan in a much different and more objective light. In his 1992 book, *Memoirs of the Ford Administration*, John Updike wrote that he uncovered "few traces of homosexual passion" when the 19th Century U.S. Senators and close friends cohabitated in various Washington, D.C. boarding homes.

Thomas J. Balcerski, Professor of History at Eastern Connecticut State University, authored the most thoroughly researched account of the relationship between King and Buchanan. In his 350-page book, *Bosom Friends: The Intimate World of James Buchanan and Rufus King*, published in September 2019, Balcerski not only closely examined King's and Buchanan's close bond but also other intimate male friendships between Antebellum-era statesmen.

Balcerski succinctly explained how common words of endearment spoken and written by men of that generation could be misconstrued by later researchers and readers as sexual in nature. Balcerski further noted male cohabitation by 19th Century statesmen was a by-product of finances and practicality while providing an environment where political coalitions were forged.

Two months after publication of *Bosom Friends*, *The Advocate*, self-promoted as the "leading source of LGBTQ+ news, since 1967," interviewed Professor Balcerski. He shared his lengthy research into the lives and times of King and Buchanan before offering a well-informed opinion.

"People are welcome to disagree, but I see very little evidence to suggest their relationship was in the least bit sexual. The strongest evidence against a sexual relationship is really the surviving evidence itself," Balcerski informed readers of *The Advocate*.

Only King and Buchanan *knew absolutely* the full details surrounding their close bond. In the 19th Century, when conviction for sodomy was punishable by lifetime imprisonment, neither man could have been expected to risk disclosure of a relationship deemed taboo by heterosexual individuals of that generation. Furthermore, members of that generation were more likely to respect professional and personal life boundaries.

By present day standards, how important is sexual orientation to the historical record? Suppose definitive proof existed that King was gay. Does the disclosure of his sexual orientation detract from his record as a statesman?

Perhaps another issue is more deserving of retrospective analysis. King was an affluent slaveholder in both North Carolina and Alabama who derived much of his wealth from back-breaking labors of human chattel.

If transported back in time to the mid-19th Century, considering our own foibles and prejudices, who among us would hold a heterosexual slaver owner in higher regard than a gay or bisexual Abolitionist?

WILLIAM R. KING'S LIFELINE

1786

King was born on April 7 in Sampson County, North Carolina.

1803

King left the University of North Carolina after three years to read for the law.

1806

King was admitted to the bar and opened his law practice in Clinton, North Carolina.

1807-08

King served in the North Carolina House of Commons.

1810

King served as Solicitor in North Carolina's Superior Court.

1811-16

King served in the U.S. House of Representatives representing the state of North Carolina.

1816-18

King served as Legation Secretary for William Pickney, American Foreign Minister to the Kingdom of the Two Sicilies and Russia.

1818

King moved to the Alabama Territory and built a home on his newly acquired King's Bend Plantation in Dallas County.

1819

King helped found a new town and personally selected the name Selma. He was elected as a delegate to the Alabama Territory's Constitutional Convention, where he served on the committee responsible for drafting the Alabama State Constitution. After Alabama was admitted to the Union, he was elected as one of the state's first two U.S. Senators.

1819-44

King served as U.S. Senator representing the state of Alabama.

1836-41

King served his first stint as President Pro Tempore of the Senate.

1844-46

King served as American Foreign Minister to France.

1848-52

King once again served as U.S. Senator representing the state of Alabama.

1850-52

King served as President Pro Tempore of the Senate, completing his combined eight-year tenure as a presiding officer.

1852

In November, King was elected 13th Vice-President of the United States.

1853

King took the Vice-Presidential oath of office on March 4 in Matanzas, Cuba.

1853

King died on April 18 at his King's Bend plantation home in Alabama.

1882

King's remains were removed from the Piney Woods family cemetery at King's Bend and reinterred in a mausoleum at Live Oak Cemetery in Selma, Alabama.

TIME LINE OF HISTORICAL EVENTS OCCURING DURING WILLIAM R. KING'S LIFETIME

1786

Andrew Meikle invented the mechanical reaper.

Charles Wilson Peale opened the American Institute of Fine Arts and Natural History.

1787

The United States Constitution was drafted, reframing the government established under the Articles of Confederation. The new government consisted of Executive, Legislative and Judicial branches.

1788

The U.S. Constitution was ratified after 9 of 13 states approved.

TIME LINE OF HISTORICAL EVENTS

1789

George Washington was unanimously elected as the first President of the United States.

Edmund Cartwright invented the power loom.

1790

The United States Supreme Court met for the first time at the Royal Exchange Building in New York City, the nation's first capital city.

The Residence Act of 1790 designated the permanent location of the United States Capital in the District of Columbia. In the interim, Philadelphia became the temporary capital city.

Thomas Saint invented the sewing machine.

1791

Pierre-Charles L'Enfant plans were accepted for design of the new capital city, Washington, D.C. The Presidential Mansion and U.S. Capitol Building were constructed on the two highest points.

The first 10 Amendments of the United States, otherwise known as the Bill of Rights, were ratified.

British clergyman and amateur geologist Revered William Gregory discovered a mineral he named Menachite. Four years later, the mineral was renamed Titanium.

1792

Architect James Hoban was selected to build the Presidential Mansion in Washington, D.C. Construction of the residence began later that year.

1793

Construction of the U.S. Capitol Building was started.

1794

Eli Whitney patented the cotton gin.

1795

Joseph Bramah invented the hydraulic press.

1796

Alois Senefelder invented lithography printing.

1797

Samuel Bentham invented plywood.

1799

George Medhurst invented the motorized air compressor.

Louis-Nicolas Robert invented the first paper machine.

1800

The United States Capital was moved from Philadelphia to Washington, D.C.

John Adams became the first President to occupy the newly constructed Presidential Mansion in Washington D.C.

Construction of the North Wing of the U.S. Capitol Building was completed and the Senate, House of Representatives, and Supreme Court occupied the structure.

TIME LINE OF HISTORICAL EVENTS

Alessandro Volta developed the first electric battery, also known as the Voltaic pile.

1801

The United Kingdom of Great Britain (England and Scotland) and Ireland was established.

1803

President Thomas Jefferson negotiated a treaty with France and the United States paid France $15,000,000 for the Louisiana Territory. As a result of the Louisiana Purchase, the U.S. added 828,000 square miles west of the Mississippi River that extended as far west as the Rocky Mountains and from the Gulf of Mexico to the Canadian border.

1804

Friederich Serturner discovered morphine as an alkaloid extract from the poppy plant.

Napoleon crowned himself Emperor of France.

1806

Meriweather Lewis and William Clark completed their Corps of Discovery three-year exploration of the Louisiana Purchase territory and located a route to the Pacific Ocean.

1807

Nicephore Niepce developed first internal combustion engine capable of performing practical work.

Robert Fulton invented the steamboat and navigated the Hudson River from New York City to Albany, New York in 32 hours (prior to that time, sailing vessels required four days to make the same journey). Humphrey Davy developed the electric arc lamp.

1810

Nicolas Appert developed food canning process.

Abraham Louis Bréguet developed first wristwatch.

1811

Friederich Koenig invented the first powered printing press.

The Presidential Mansion in Washington, D.C. was first called "The White House."

1812

The War of 1812 began.

William Reid Clanny invented the safety lamp.

1814

British troops occupied Washington, D.C. and burned most structures, including the President's Mansion, Capitol Building, and Treasury Building.

Francis Scott Key composed The Star Bangled Banner after viewing the battered American flag hoisted above Fort McHenry, Maryland as British ships withdrew from Baltimore near the end of the War of 1812.

George Stephenson built the first steam locomotive.

1815

The Battle of Waterloo was fought, ending Napoleon's career.

TIME LINE OF HISTORICAL EVENTS

1816

Rene Laennec invented the stethoscope.

1818

Architect Charles Bullfinch was awarded the contract to rebuild the U.S. Capitol Building.

Frankenstein by Mary Shelly was published.

1819

Spain ceded the Florida Territory to the U.S.

1820

The Missouri Compromise was passed by Congress and signed into law by President James Monroe.

1821

The U.S. began formal occupation of the Florida Territory and future President Andrew Jackson appointed Territorial Governor.

1823

President James Monroe issued the Monroe Doctrine, warning European countries not to establish colonies in the Americas.

1824

The Bureau of Indian Affairs was established.

Johann Nikolas von Dreyse invented the bolt-action rifle.

1825

The Erie Canal between the Hudson River and Lake Erie opened. Over 300-miles-long, the waterway connected the East Coast with the developing frontier.

1826

Former Presidents John Adams and Thomas Jefferson died on July 4, the 50th anniversary of the signing of the Declaration of Independence.

The Last of the Mohicans by James Fenimore Cooper was published.

James Sharp developed the first practical gas stove.

John Walker developed the friction match.

1827

Joseph Nicephore Niepce developed the first modern photograph.

1828

Andrew Jackson was elected President of the United States, and the Democratic Party was formed.

Patrick Bell invented the reaping machine.

Odes and Ballads by Victor Hugo published.

1829

Louis Braille invented the Braille reading system for the blind.

1830

The Indian Removal Act authorized the federal government to negotiate treaties with Native American tribes in the eastern U.S. in exchange for their removal west of the Mississippi River.

Edwin Budding invented the lawn mower.

TIME LINE OF HISTORICAL EVENTS

1831

Cyrus McCormick invented the mechanical reaper.

Chloroform was first synthesized.

1834

Moritz von Jacobi invented the first practical electric motor.

1836

Texas became an independent republic after winning independence from Mexico.

Samuel Colt patented the revolver which could be fired multiple times without reloading.

1837

Samuel Morse patented the electric telegraph, America's first long-distance communication device.

Victoria was crowned Queen of the United Kingdom.

1839

Charles Goodyear perfected durable vulcanized rubber.

William Otis invented the steam shovel.

1842

William Robert Grove invented the first fuel cell.

Ulysses by Alfred Lord Tennyson was published.

1844

Francis Rynd invented the hypodermic needle.

1845

Narrative of the Life of Frederick Douglass an American Slave by Frederick Douglass was published.

1846

The Mexican-American War began.

The Smithsonian Institute was established, named in honor of British-born scientist James Smithson.

1847

Ascanio Sobrero invented nitroglycerin, the first explosive more powerful than black powder.

Jane Eyre by Charlotte Bronte published.

1848

The Treaty of Guadalupe Hidalgo was signed, ending the Mexican-American War. Under the terms of the treaty, the U.S. paid $15,000,000 to Mexico which ceded 500,000 square miles of land in the west and southwest. In addition, the Rio Grande River was established as the border between the U.S. and Mexico.

Gold was discovered on Colonel John Sutter's property on the South Fork of the American River in Coloma, California, initiating the "California Gold Rush."

Jonathan J. Couch invented the pneumatic drill.

Linus Yale Sr. invented the modern tumbler lock.

TIME LINE OF HISTORICAL EVENTS

Wuthering Heights by Emily Bronte was published.

The Communist Manifesto by Karl Marx and Friedrich Engels was published.

1849

James Francis invented the water turbine to be later used in hydropower plants.

Walter Hunt invented the first repeating rifle to use metallic cartridges and utilize a spring-fed magazine. That same year, Hunt invented the safety pin.

1850

The Compromise of 1850 was passed, once again easing sectional conflict over slavery.

The Scarlet Letter by Nathaniel Hawthorne was published.

1851

Moby Dick by Herman Melville published.

George Jennings developed the first public flush toilets which cost one-cent-per-visit.

1852

Uncle Tom's Cabin by Harriet Beecher Stowe published.

Elisha Otis invented the safety break elevator.

Henri Gifford made the first manned flight in a dirigible.

BIBLIOGRAPHY

Internet resources:

www.encyclopediaofalabama.org

www.alabamalegacy.org

www.history.com

www.ncpedia.org

www.loc.gov

www.worldcat.org

www.bioguide.congress.gov

www.alabamamoments.state.al.us

www.openlibrary.org

www.senate.gov

www.api.semanticscholar.org

www.pubmed.ncbi.nl

www.cdc.gov/tb

www.cspan.org

BIBLIOGRAPHY

www.millercenter.org

www.theadvocate.com

www.web.archive.org

www.findagrave.com

www.seattletimes.com

www.alabamaheritage.com

www.nchistoricalreview.com

www.alabamareview.com

www.filesusgwarchives.net

www.clintonnc.com

www.thebump.com

www.sampsonnc.com

www.ncdcr.gov

www.aoc.gov

www.jeffcohistory.com

www.your.kingcounty.gov

www.dailymail.co.uk

www.loc.gov/pictures

www.worldcat.org

www.home.treasury.gov

www.ushistory.org

www.thoughtco.com

www.battlefields.org

www.usconstitutionmuseum.org

www.whitehouse.gov

www.ourcampaigns.com

www.countingthevotes.com

www.avalon.law.yale.edu

www.ourdocuments.gov

www.tamu.edu

www.census.gov

www.academic.udayton.edu

www.explorebaltimoreheritage.org

www.buchananlumbermobile.com

www.dpi.nc.gov

www.nationalgeographic.org

www.norton.com

www.gsa.gov

www.loc.gov

www.americanexperience.si.edu

Books:

Appleby, Joyce. *Inheriting the Revolution: The First Generation of Americans.* Harvard University Press, 2000.

Bailey, Tom. *William Rufus King: Alabama's U.S. Vice-President.* Seacoast Publishing, 2002.

Balcerski, Thomas J. *Bosom Friends: The Intimate World of James Buchanan & William Rufus King.* Oxford University Press, 2019.

Barzman, Sol. *Madmen & Geniuses: The Vice-Presidents of the United States.* Follet Publishing, 1974.

Beneman, William. *Male-Male Intimacy in Early America:*

BIBLIOGRAPHY

Beyond Romantic Relationships. Routledge, 2006.

Carnes, Mark C., and Clyde Griffin, eds. *Meaning for Manhood: Constructions of Masculinity in Victorian America*. University of Chicago Press, 1990.

Cincotta, Howard, ed, et. al. *An Outline of American History*. United States Information Agency, 1994

Cowen, David. *The Origins and Economic Impact of the First Bank of the United States, 1791-1797*. Garland Publishing, 2000.

Crapol, Edward. *John Tyler: The Accidental President*. University of North Carolina Press, 2002.

Ferri, F. F. *Ferri's Differential Diagnosis: A Practical Guide to the Differential Diagnosis of Symptoms, Signs, and Clinical Disorders, 2nd Edition*. Elsevier/Mosby, 2010.

Foner, Eric. *Free Soil, Free Labor, Free Men: The Ideology of the Republican Party Before the Civil War*. Oxford University Press, 1955.

Good, Cassandra. *Founding Friendships: Friendships Between Men and Women in the Early American Republic*. Oxford University Press, 2015.

Green, Michael D. *The Politics of Indian Removal: Creek Government and Society in Crisis*. University of Nebraska Press, 1982.

Hammond, Bray. *Banks & Politics in America from the Revolution to the Civil War*. Princeton University Press, 1957.

Harris, R. E. *Epidemiology of Chronic Disease: Global Perspectives*. Jones & Bartlett Learning, 2013.

Henderson, Timothy. *A Glorious Defeat: Mexico and its War with the United States*. Hill and Wong, 2007.

Holt, Michael F. *Political Parties and American Political Development from the Age of Jackson to the Age of Lincoln.* Louisiana State University Press, 1992.

Jackson, Walter M. *Alabama's First United States Vice-President: William Rufus King.* Decatur Printing Company, 1952.

Kluger, Richard. *Seizing Destiny: How America Grew from Sea to Shining Sea.* Knopf, 2007.

Lewis, Herbert James. *Alabama Founders: Fourteen Political and Military Leaders Who Shaped the State.* University of Alabama Press, 2018.

Morgan, Robert. *Lions of the West: Heroes and Villains of the Westward Expansion.* Algonquin Books, 2012.

Nowland, Robert A. *The American Presidents from Polk to Hayes.* Outskirts Press, 2016.

Patrick, John J., Richard M. Pious, and Donald A. Ritchie, eds. *The Oxford Guide to the United States Government.* Oxford University Press, 2021.

Purcell, L. Edward, ed. *Vice-Presidents: A Biographical Dictionary.* Facts on File Publishing, 2005.

Rayback, Joseph G. *Free Soil: The Election of 1848.* University of Kentucky Press, 2015.

Smith, Elbert B. *President Zachary Taylor: The Hero President.* Nova Scotia Pub, 20.

Smith, Jeffrey K. *The Loyalist: The Life and Times of Andrew Johnson.* CreateSpace, 2012.

Smith, Jeffrey K. *Rendezvous in Dallas: The Assassination of John F. Kennedy.* CreateSpace, 2012.

Smith, Jeffrey K. *The Presidential Assassins: John Wilkes Booth,*

BIBLIOGRAPHY

Charles Julius Guiteau, Leon Frank Czolgosz, and Lee Harvey Oswald. CreateSpace, 2013.

Smith Jeffrey K. *You Were Right and We Were Wrong: The Life and Times of Judge Frank M. Johnson, Jr.* CreateSpace, 2016.

Smith, Jeffrey K. *A Prelude to War: The Presidency of James Buchanan*. Outskirts Press, 2019.

Smith, Jeffrey K. *Freedom and Opportunity: Robert Smalls and the End of Slavery in America*, Palmetto Publishing, 2023.

Stewart, John Craig. *The Governors of Alabama*. Pelican Publishing Company, 1975.

Watson, Elbert L. *Alabama United States Senators*. Strode Publishers,1982.

Webb, Samuel L. and Margaret F. Armbrester. *Alabama Governors: A Political History of the State*. The University of Alabama Press, 2001.

Whitney, David C., revised and updated by Robin Vaughn Whitney. *The American Presidents: Biographies of Our Chief Executives, 4th edition*. Madison Park Press, 2009.

Widmer, Edward L. *Martin Van Buren*. Times Books, 2005.

Wilentz, Sean. *The Rise of American Democracy: Jefferson to Lincoln*. W. W. Norton and Company, 2008.

Windham, Kathryn Tucker. *Alabama: One Big Front Porch*. New South Books, 2019.

ACKNOWLEDGEMENTS

I sincerely hope readers found the latest narrative in my "Bringing History Alive Series" entertaining and informative. As always, your time, interest, and support are most appreciated.

The efforts of many researchers and writers predated this book. I am most grateful to those, living and dead, referenced in the bibliography.

I owe special gratitude to journalist and editor, Ricky Adams, who once again endeavored to make my words more readable. Thank you, my friend.

I am once again indebted to my sister and talented artist, Elaine Kerr. Her cover image depicts William R. King's final resting place in Selma, Alabama, the town he not only helped found but also named. I love you, Sis.

Anne, my wife of over 36 years, lends support and encouragement to a full-time physician and part-time writer. I love you very much.

Our sons and daughters-in law, Andy and Abbey and Ben and Polly, are the lights of my life. I love you more than I can put into words.

I dedicate this book to my late brother-in-law, J. Brice Kerr. He taught me much, enriched my life with laughter, and was a masterful story teller. Brice, I love and miss you very much.

If readers have questions or comments about this narrative or my earlier works, please feel free to contact me (newfrontierpublications @

ACKNOWLEDGEMENTS

gmail.com). Your feedback is most welcome. If you have the time and inclination to post a book review on Amazon, Goodreads, or other forums, the author would be most appreciative. I am always honored to give presentations and appear at book signings when possible.

ABOUT THE AUTHOR

Jeffrey K. Smith is a physician and author. A native of Enterprise, Alabama, he earned his undergraduate and medical degrees from the University of Alabama. After completing residency training at the William S. Hall Psychiatric Institute (now known as the University of South Carolina Department of Neuropsychiatry and Behavioral Science), he entered private practice in Upstate South Carolina. Along with his wife, Anne, they reside in Greer, South Carolina. They are the proud parents of two sons and daughters-in-law as well as a pair of beloved and spoiled dogs.

Dr. Smith is the author of three murder mystery novels and 20 works of non-fiction. The latter narratives represent his "Bringing History Alive" series.

OTHER BOOKS BY JEFFREY K. SMITH

Fiction:

Sudden Despair
Two Down, Two To Go
A Phantom Killer

Non-fiction:

Rendezvous in Dallas: The Assassination of John F. Kennedy (two editions)

The Fighting Little Judge: The Life and Times of George C. Wallace

Fire in the Sky: The Story of the Atomic Bomb

Bad Blood: Lyndon B. Johnson, Robert F. Kennedy and the Tumultuous 1960s (two editions)

Dixiecrat: The Life and Times of Strom Thurmond

The Loyalist: The Life and Times of Andrew Johnson

The Eagle Has Landed: The Story of Apollo 11

The Presidential Assassins: John Wilkes Booth, Charles Julius Guiteau, Leon Frank Czolgosz, and Lee Harvey Oswald

The War on Crime: J. Edgar Hoover Versus the John Dillinger Gang

The Wizard of the Saddle: General Nathan Bedford Forrest

You Were Right and We Were Wrong: The Life and Times of Judge Frank M. Johnson, Jr.

Grover Cleveland: The Last Conservative Democratic President

Listen To Me: The Brief Life and Enduring Legacy of Buddy Holly

A Family Affair: The Rosenberg Espionage Case

A Prelude to War: The Presidency of James Buchanan

The Assistant President: South Carolina's James F. Byrnes

A Lingering Evil: The Unsolved Murder of Buford Lolley

A Pea River Progeny: Alabama's Colorful and Controversial Governor James E. "Big Jim" Folsom

Freedom and Opportunity: Robert Smalls and the End of Slavery in America

Milton Keynes UK
Ingram Content Group UK Ltd.
UKHW030150051224
452010UK00010B/582